Word 97 Basic Skills

Sue Coles

Department of Business and Management Studies
Crewe and Alsager Faculty
Manchester Metropolitan University

Jenny Rowley

School of Management and Social Sciences
Edge Hill University College

Letts
1997

Acknowledgments

This book would not have been completed without the support that the authors received, during its production, from many of their colleagues and family. They are particularly grateful to husbands Martyn and Peter, children Helen, Shula, Lynsey and Zeta, who had to make do with even less of their time than usual.

Windows 95™ and Access™ © Microsoft Corporation, all rights reserved. Screen displays from Access 7 and Windows 95 reprinted with permission from Microsoft Corporation.

A CIP record for this book is available from the British Library.

ISBN 1 85805 221 1

Editorial and production services: Genesys Editorial Limited

Typeset by Kai, Nottingham

Printed in Great Britain by Ashford Colour Press, Gosport

Contents

About this book

Aims

This book introduces the basics of Word 97 and progresses to an intermediate level in a single reasonably priced volume. The book assumes no prior experience of any word processing package.

This book is written for people who are new to Word 97, which is an industry standard word processing package. You can use it

- as part of a college course
- for independent study
- for reference.

Although the book uses a business oriented approach for the practical activities this approach will be easily adaptable to other situations where documents for other purposes, such as assignments or projects, are being produced.

You may also wish to further your word processing skills using Word 97 by reading **Word 97 Further Skills**, which builds on the material presented in this volume.

A note to lecturers and students

This book introduces students to the basics of word processing through a series of applications orientated exercises. The approach is structured to focus on the end product, whether that product be a letter, memo, advertisement, curriculum vitae, project report, thesis or other document. A series of self-contained sessions takes students through the production of various document types and gradually introduces them to the features and functions of the word processing package. Each session comprises a series of exercises, As each new function is introduced, the book explains both why the function is useful and how to use it.

The approach is designed not only to introduce students to Word but also to offer them a conceptual framework for word processing that will facilitate the development of transferable skills.

The learning material requires little, if any, input by lecturers, and can therefore be used in programmes based on independent learning. Students learn by practising the commands and techniques to produce specific types of documents.

Word for Windows is a sophisticated package including many desktop publishing type features, a graphics package and a draw package. The text is selective and does not deal with all of these in detail, but does take students step-by-step to a level at which they can happily use the help system or software manual to master further features.

The exercises follow a theme. Many, but not all, of the exercises lead towards the creation of a student report. This report is concerned with the development of a new fitness facility in a leisure centre. In order to minimise the amount of keying necessary to complete the exercises, early exercises create documents that are reused later in the book. By Unit 12 various earlier documents will be drawn together to produce a project report. Later sessions deal with specific topics and facilities that may be used to enhance the report further or that may be used in alternative contexts such as the creation of a newsletter.

In Word there are often many ways of achieving the same operation. This book offers the quickest and most user friendly means of achieving set objectives. Although at times other methods may also be indicated, preference is given to operations based on the use of the mouse and menu options. This approach makes maximum use of the self-explanatory nature of the menu options and dialog boxes, and does not ask the user to remember key combinations. Key combinations are indicated against menu options in the system, and users may familiarise themselves with these as their experience in using the software develops.

Getting started

Students who have not used a Windows program before should first read through Quick Reference 1 **Basic Windows Operations**, which summarises the key features of the Windows environment, and then turn to **An overview of Word for Windows** before tackling Unit 1. Students who are familiar with the Windows environment should also read through **An overview of Word for Windows** before beginning Unit 1.

Students can refer to Quick Reference 2 **Buttons on the toolbars** whenever they need reminding of the functions of each button on the toolbars. Quick Reference 3 **Customising Word** is intended for

- those whose Word system has been customised so that it does not use the default settings assumed in this book (students should ask lecturers to perform the necessary commands to return their system to its default setting)

- those students who, having worked through all the units in the book, feel confident enough to create their own settings for Word.

Conventions

The following conventions have been adopted to distinguish between the various objects on the screen:

- On-screen buttons and icon names are shown as **Cancel** .

- Menu items and dialog boxes are shown as **File-Open**.

- Filenames, names of fields, documents or any thing else named by the user are shown as: **Termref**.

- Text which you are instructed to type in yourself is shown in Times typeface which looks like this.

- Keys on the keyboard are shown as *Ctrl*.

indicates a tip providing a helpful hint or short-cut method.

 indicates a cautionary note.

 indicates a cross reference.

An overview of Word 97

What you will learn in this section

All readers (except those who have some experience of Word for Windows) should read this section before tackling Unit 1. Quick Reference 1 reviews the basic features of Windows 95 for the benefit of inexperienced users or as a ready reference for those who may have forgotten some of the basic features. Quick Reference 1 also introduces mouse techniques and acts as a summary of the terminology used elsewhere in this book. At the end of this unit you should

- be familiar with the basic elements of the Word screen
- know about the Office Assistant and be aware of how to use Word's help facilities.

A tour of the Word for Windows screen

It is worth studying the Word for Windows screen for a few moments before trying to make use of it. There is rather a lot of information summarised in the next two pages. A quick read should serve to orientate you, but do not expect to remember all of this detail. This section can be used as a ready reference and returned to as necessary.

The Word screen can be formatted in a number of different ways. To make sure that you are looking at the same screen as described in this text, choose **View-Ruler**, to switch on a tick ✓ against **Ruler**. From the **View** menu move the mouse pointer over **Toolbars** and check that there are ticks ✓ by the **Standard** and **Formatting** toolbars.

Now choose **Tools-Options**, then the **View** tab, and make sure that there are ticks against **Horizontal scroll bar** and **Status bar**.

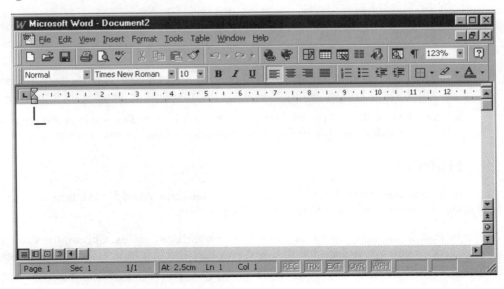

The Word screen that you should now be viewing has the following components.

■ **Title bar**: shows the name of the document (or Documentx if you have yet to name the document).

■ **Word control menu**: in the very top left-hand corner. If you click on this symbol a menu with commands for sizing and moving the Word window, and closing Word, is displayed.

■ **Document control menu**: in the top left-hand corner, but below the Word control menu. If you click on this symbol a menu with commands for sizing, moving and closing the document is displayed.

■ **Word main menu**: shows the main pull-down menus, File, Edit, View, Insert, Format, Tools, Table, Window and Help.

■ **Standard toolbar**: shows a series of buttons which can be used to perform some commands quickly. The actions of the buttons are listed in Quick Reference 2. If you point to a button for several seconds a small box appears showing its name, which gives an idea of its function.

■ **Formatting toolbar**: shows the character and paragraph formatting in force at the current position of the insertion point. It displays character formatting such as font, size, and whether it is bold, italics and so on, and paragraph formatting such as left or right justification. On the left of this toolbar are the font and point size boxes. To the right is a series of buttons. The meaning of these buttons is shown in Quick Reference 2.

The font and point size can be changed by clicking on the list box down arrow to drop down a list of alternatives, and by clicking on one of them. The buttons on the right show the current state of the text and allow it to be changed. For example, to change characters to italic it is necessary to select the characters and click the italic button. The italic button goes in and stays in while the cursor is moving over italic characters.

On the left of the toolbar is the style box, which indicates the style that has been used to format the selection. Styles allow you to format your document more easily.

■ **Ruler**: gives information about the indentation and tab stops of the selected paragraph. Indents appear as tiny triangles, tabs as shapes indicating their function

■ **Status bar**: at the bottom of the screen. It gives information such as the page number and section number of the current location of the insertion point.

Help

Both help and examples and demos are available for Word for Windows. There are four main methods of getting into the help system.

1 Pull down the Help menu and select Contents and Index. Choose the Contents tab if you are looking for an overview of a particular topic. Choose the Index tab to look up a specific item.

2   At any time you can press the F1 key to get help on whatever you are doing at that moment via the Office Assistant.

3   In many dialog boxes there is a **Help** button on the title bar. Click on this then click on the item in the dialog box for which you require extra information.

4   Press *Shift/F1*. The pointer changes to an arrow with a question mark after it and it can be used to point to anything. Clicking on that object will then bring up help. For instance, in this way you may get help on the meaning of all of the items in a particular toolbar.

The Office Assistant

Click on the Office Assistant button to display the Office Assistant. The Office Assistant is an animated graphic that appears in a window of its own, and if your PC has a sound card it also alerts your attention using various sounds. When you have a question about how to do something you can ask the Office Assistant, for example, 'How do I print in landscape?'. To do this click on the Assistant window, key your question into the **What would you like to do?** box and click on the **Search** button.

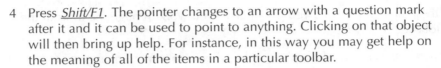

 The Assistant can, if you wish, provide help with tasks as you perform them without the need to ask questions.

You can choose an Assistant to match your personality and as the Assistant is shared by the suite of Office programs, it will be a familiar guide when you are working with an application other than Word. Using the Office CD-ROM, you may select a different assistant, by clicking on the Assistant and choosing one.

Task 1: Using help

This task encourages you to explore the help system and to start to use the Word window.

1   Click on the **Help** menu on the Word main menu. This should cause the pull-down menu to be displayed. Click on **Contents and Index** to open the **Help Topics: Microsoft Word** window.

2   Choose the **Index** tab and enter an item, for example 'printing' into box 1. Click on **Display** . Read the help information displayed.

3   When you have finished close this window by clicking on the cross in the upper right-hand corner of the window (if you are not sure where this is consult Quick Reference 1).

4   Try choosing the **Contents** tab and looking up spelling and grammar.

5 Click on the Office Assistant and ask 'How do I print in landscape?'.

6 You may like to click on Office Assistant's **Options** button and customise your assistant.

Ten basic tips

Use these tips to refer to if you get stuck as you work through the tasks in the units that follow.

1 Always *select*, then *do*. For example, when you want to change text, first select it and then choose a command or click on a button that will do what you want.

2 Save your document regularly, say every 5 to 10 minutes. The fastest way to save is to click on the **Save** button on the standard toolbar or to press *Ctrl/s*.

3 If you do not like what you have just done, undo it using Edit-Undo or by clicking on the **Undo** button in the toolbar. Word will allow you to undo more than one operation.

4 Press *F1* to call the Office Assistant for help.

5 Do not press *Enter* at the end of every line. Only press *Enter* at the end of a paragraph.

6 Do make full use of the table feature to create tables.

7 Do not use the *Spacebar* to create indents. Set indents by using the ruler, or **Format-Paragraph**, or the **Indent** button on the formatting toolbar.

8 Use the standard toolbar to complete most common tasks.

9 Use the formatting toolbar to apply formatting to your document.

10 Use the ruler to adjust margins, tab settings and table columns.

Basics of document creation

What you will learn in this unit

In this unit basic operations that are fundamental to the effective use of Word are introduced. At the end of this unit you will be able to

- enter Word for Windows

- create a simple document

- save a document

- close a document

- exit Word for Windows

- use Word's aids to typing.

Such operations will allow you to construct simple letters and memos.

The simple documents created in this unit can be further improved by the use of other facilities described in subsequent units.

The operations covered in this unit are essential to the successful creation of any document. For example, it is essential to be confident that you have saved a document before going on to create longer or more sophisticated documents.

Once you are familiar with Word for Windows, you will perform most of the operations covered in this and the next unit again and again. The sequence adopted in this unit is significant. Always remember to save a document after you have created it and before performing other operations, such as printing.

When you have completed this and the next unit you will have grasped some important basics. Word for Windows has a number of default settings, such as A4 paper size and specified margins, which you may wish to adjust later in order to change the document's appearance, but for this unit you should accept the default settings. These default settings usually allow you to create your first documents very painlessly.

Creating a simple new document

This exercise takes you into Word for Windows, and asks you to open a new document, type in a simple letter and make corrections.

Entering Word for Windows

To enter Word for Windows double click on the Word for Windows icon in its program group.

In Windows 95 it is convenient to drag the Word icon onto your desktop, then you can click on this shortcut icon to launch Word. While the software is loading the pointer will be displayed as an egg timer. Word for Windows will open with a new document ready for you to enter text. The screen should show the basic Word screen (as in the Overview), with an empty document automatically open for you.

Entering text

Text can be entered via the keyboard. The only important difference between word processing and typing at this stage is that you should not press the *Enter* key at the end of a line. Instead, if you continue typing, the text wraps automatically onto the new line. If you do press the *Enter* key this will prevent the effective formatting of documents later. *Enter* should only be pressed when you wish to commence a new paragraph, or to execute a command.

Making running corrections

Simple corrections of one or two characters or words can be made by placing the insertion point beside the character to be amended. Note that Word marks words that it cannot find in its dictionary with a wavy underline but do not worry too much about this at first as spelling will be covered later.

The insertion point can be positioned by

- positioning the mouse pointer where you want the insertion point to be and clicking

- pressing the arrow keys.

Remember that you cannot position the insertion point past the end mark at the end of a document.

Next apply whichever of the following is appropriate

- the *Backspace* key to delete characters to the left of the cursor

- the *Delete* key to delete characters to the right of the cursor

- key in additional characters.

Task 1: Creating a new document

1 Enter Word for Windows.

2 Type in the simple letter shown below. Do not forget that you should not press *Enter* at the end of each line unless a new paragraph is required.

Make any necessary running corrections.

Chelmer Leisure and Recreation Centre
Park View Road
Chelmer
Cheshire
CE9 1JS

Universal Gym (Europe) Ltd
Hutton
Brentwood
Essex
CM13 1XA

17 October 1996

Dear Sir

Health and Fitness Centre for Chelmer Leisure and Recreation Centre.

As part of my studies for my BA in Business Studies, Sport and Recreation, I am
conducting a project on behalf of Chelmer Leisure and Recreation Centre.

Chelmer Leisure and Recreation Centre wishes to investigate the options for the
enhancement of their health and fitness facilities. Currently I am approaching a
number of potential suppliers with a view to collecting information on the range of
equipment available in the marketplace. I would therefore be grateful if you would
supply me with appropriate publicity literature and equipment specifications,
together with price lists.

Thank you

Yours faithfully

Ms S Leveridge.

Once you have created the letter move on to Task 2, which asks you to save the
letter for later use.

Saving a document

To save a document use **File-Save** or click on the ▮ **Save** ▮ button on the toolbar.
The first time a new document is being saved this will bring the **Save As** dialog box

 onto the screen as shown below.

3

This contains the following boxes.

- **Save in:** This shows the name of the currently selected directory. This needs to be the directory in which you wish to save your file. The arrow allows you to display the directory structure, which shows the structure above that of the currently displayed directory.

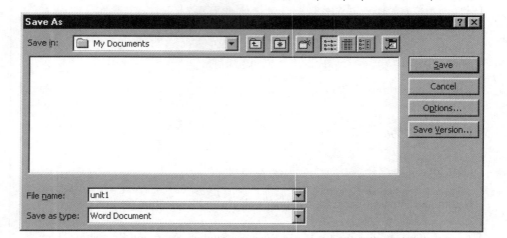

- **File name:** This shows the names of the files in the current directory, these being any other documents that you may have created. **File name:** displays the current default name, for example, **Doc1** or an earlier name of the file. You can either accept this or click in the box to modify it.

- **Save as type:** This shows the different types of file formats that you may choose to save your file as. Usually the default, Word document, is acceptable.

For your first document it should be sufficient to enter the filename in the **File name:** box, and click on **Save** or press *Enter*.

Once you have saved a document it may be saved on subsequent occasions by using **File-Save**.

 It is good practice to save a long document every twenty minutes or so. Certainly make sure that you save every document before attempting to print it. Word offers an autosaving function, which is described in Quick Reference 3.

More on filenames

Traditionally, filenames for Word documents were from one to eight characters in length, followed by, optionally, a period and a one to three character filename extension. Now, however, Word allows you to use long descriptive filenames. The complete path to the file, including drive letter, folder path name and filename, can contain up to 255 characters. If you do not understand this statement we suggest that you use short filenames.

Any characters may be used except the following: * ? ; \ / : " | < >. You cannot use a period except to separate the filename from the extension.

Filename extensions are usually used to distinguish between different types of files. For example, document files generally have the extension **.doc**, backup files have the extension **.bak**, and if you have any spreadsheet files created with Excel these will have the extension **,xls**. Generally, there is no need to type the extension because Word automatically adds **.doc**. In Windows 95 the file extension is not usually shown, for instance in the Open and Save dialog boxes, although it is there.

Instead you will see a Word document icon next to the filename.

Choose meaningful filenames so that you can easily retrieve your documents later.

Task 2: Saving

To save the document that you created in Task 1 as Letter1

1 Click on **File-Save**.

2 Enter **Letter1** in the **File name:** box. **Save**

3 Click on **Save** .   The file is saved.

If you wish to save more than one version of a document, you may save the later version of the document under a different filename, as discussed in the next unit.

Closing documents and exiting from Word

Once you have finished working on a document and have saved it you may wish to close it. Closing a document is the equivalent of putting the document away in a manual system. All documents must be closed before exiting Word. If you try to exit with unsaved documents open, Word will ask you if you wish to save and close them. In a Windows application such as Word you may have a number of document windows open at any one time. It is not necessary to close one document before opening a different or new document in a different window. But new Windows users should be wary of opening too many documents at once. It is easy to convince yourself that you have lost your work when it is merely on a hidden window. So, to start with, close all documents as you finish with them. Documents can be closed by selecting **File-Close** or by double clicking on the document control menu box in the upper left corner of the document window. When you have closed all documents the application background appears.

When you wish to leave Word, choose **File-Exit**. Alternatively, you may double click on the control menu box at the top left of the screen and select Close, or use the keyboard shortcut *Alt/f4*.

Task 3: Closing and exiting

1   Close the document, **Letter1**, using   The document is closed, leaving no
    File-Close.   documents open in Word.

2   Exit from Word by choosing **File-Exit**.

Using Word's aids to typing

As you type in a document Word will try to recognise some common text
that you type, for example, the days of the week, months of the year, the
month and year of a date and your name (if it knows that you are the
owner of the software). As you type the word, Word will guess the completed word
and display it in a small box above your typing. Press *Enter* to accept the completed
word. If you do not want the word suggested then continue typing and it will disappear.

 Word maintains a list of common words that you type, to provide you with these
shortcuts, which is known as AutoText. Unit 6 introduces AutoText and you will see
how to add words and phrases to the AutoText list.

Task 4: Using AutoText

1   Start Word and open a new docu-
    ment by clicking on the **New**
    button in the toolbar or by using **File-
    New** and choosing blank document.

    Blank
    Document

2   Try typing in the days of the week and the months of the year. Practise accepting
    or ignoring the completed word.

3   Close the document without saving
    by using **File-Close** and answering
    '**no**' to the Office Assistant. Exit from
    Word by choosing **File-Exit**.

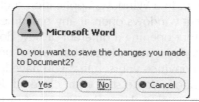

Basics of document control

What you will learn in this unit

In this unit basic operations that are fundamental to the effective control of documents are introduced. At the end of this unit you will be able to

- open a document
- edit a document
- print a document.

In this unit you will open an existing document, make appropriate amendments and save the amended document under a different filename. By doing this an extra document is created which is a modified version of the original, yet the original document is unchanged. Normally, documents are saved with the same name following revision, using **File-Save**, but as Task 1 illustrates **File-Save As** can create a copy of the document file with either a new name and/or saved in a different location.

What you should know already

Before you start this unit, make sure you can do the following.

Skill	Covered in
Create and save a document	Unit 1

What you need

To complete this unit you will need

- the document file **Letter1** created in Unit 1.

Opening a document

To open an existing document, use **File Open** or click on the **Open** button on the standard toolbar. This causes the **Open** dialog box to be displayed.

The **Open** dialog box has a similar layout to the **Save As** dialog box. Click on an appropriate filename then click on **Open**, or alternatively double click on the filename. If there are more files than can be displayed in the box, either click on the down arrow or drag the scroll box to view the other filenames.

Insert and overwrite

Normally you use the word processor in insert mode; that is, the existing text is moved along to make room for any new text. By double clicking on the **OVR** button on the status bar at the bottom of the screen you can change to the overwrite mode, which will allow you to type over existing text. To return to insert mode double click on the **OVR** button again. The letters **OVR** in the status bar appear black when you are in overwrite mode and grey in insert mode.

Saving another copy

An additional copy of a document can be saved, simply by choosing **File-Save As** and entering a new filename. This will create two copies of the document under different names. Alternatively, two copies may be stored under the same name, but in different drives or directories. For example, you may wish to save an additional copy to floppy disk by changing to the 3.5 Floppy (A:) drive when saving. To switch to a different drive and/or directory, in the **Save As** dialog box, open the **Save in** drop down list box, select the desired drive and directory and click on **Save**.

Task 1: Opening and editing a document

This task creates a second updated version of the document **Letter1** while keeping the first version.

1   Start Word for Windows.

2   Open the document that you saved as **Letter1** in Task 2 of Unit 1, by using **File-Open** and selecting this file from the list displayed.
    Check that you have selected the drive and directory in which you saved the file.

3   Add the following paragraph at the end of the text of the letter, before 'Thank you'.

    I shall contact you again within a few weeks for more detailed discussions if the Leisure and Recreation Centre Manager feels that your equipment might meet our requirements.

4   Save the new file using **File-Save As**, but this time using the filename **Letter2**.

5   Close the document **Letter2**.
    You should now have two files, called **Letter1**, and **Letter2**, respectively. Using **File-Open** again inspect the **File name:** box to check that this is the case.

6   Click on **Cancel** to close the dialog box.

Printing a document

You will normally print a document when it is open and being displayed on your screen. You should always view your document in **Print Preview** before printing, in order to check the general layout of the page. The quickest way to create a printed copy is to issue the **File-Print Preview** command (or click on the **Print Preview** button), and then, once in Print Preview, click on the **Print** button.

Using **File-Print** from either the document view or the print preview will bring up the **Print** dialog box. Usually you can safely accept all of the default settings, so just click on **OK**, and, provided that your printer is on, loaded with paper and on-line, printing will commence.

This is a very simple approach to printing. Below we briefly review some of the options available in printing. There are a number of parameters that can be set. You may wish to skip these for now and return to them later. These parameters are set under the **Print Preview**, **Page Setup**, **Page Layout** and **Print Setup** options. These are outlined below.

Print Preview screen

All documents should be viewed either using **Print Preview** on the **File** menu, or the **Page Layout** command on the **View** menu, before being printed.

The Print Preview screen has the following buttons in its toolbar.

Print Clicking this will print one copy of a document quickly using the current print settings.

Magnifier allows you to zoom in and zoom out.

One Page displays only one page of the document at a time.

Use *Page Up* and *Page Down* to move through the pages of your document.

Multiple Pages allows you to switch between the display of two or more pages on the screen.

Zoom controls how large or small a document appears on the screen. You can enlarge the display to make it easier to read or reduce the display to view an entire page.

View Rulers displays vertical and horizontal rulers for adjusting the top, bottom, left and right margins. These can be adjusted by dragging the markers on the rulers.

Shrink to Fit if only a few lines of your document appear on the last page, you may be able to reduce the number of pages using this option.

Full Screen expands the document to fill the screen. Click on this button to display only the previewed page(s) and the Print Preview toolbar. To display all elements click on this button again.

Close Preview closes the Print Preview screen and returns you to your document view.

Context Sensitive Help Click on this to create a Help pointer. Click the Help pointer on any item on the screen to display help information.

Print dialog box

The **Print** dialog box is displayed when the **File-Print** command is used. It allows a number of options to be set. These include

- printer details: the current printer is shown, together with details about its status, type etc. Opening this drop-down list will allow you to select an alternative printer if there is more than one printer available

- the **Properties** button takes you to the **Properties** dialog box. Through this dialog box you may choose from a range of printing options offered by your printer, such as print quality, media size, and landscape or portrait orientation

- **Page Range:** shows which sections of the document are to be printed, either all, current page, selection (if one is made) or specified pages

- **Print what:** shows the document type

- **Copies:** shows the number of copies to be printed, and whether they are to be collated

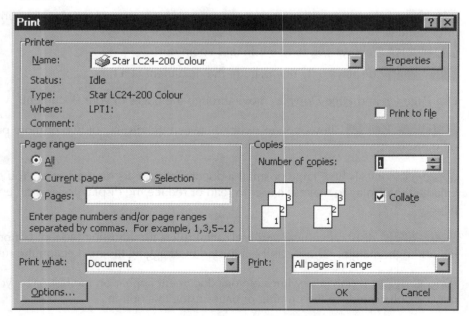

- **Print:** this drop-down list allows the choice between all pages, odd pages or even pages to be made. If you wish to print double-sided then this can be achieved by printing all of the odd pages, putting the paper back in the printer, reversed, and printing all of the even pages

- The ▐ **Options** ▐ button takes you to the **Options** dialog box. The **Options** dialog box offers a range of more specialised printing options such as draft output, reverse print order or print hidden text.

Page Setup

Page Setup, on the **File** menu, allows you to set a number of parameters, which specify how the document will be displayed on the page. Four main options are available

- **Margins**
- **Paper Size**
- **Paper Source**
- **Layout**.

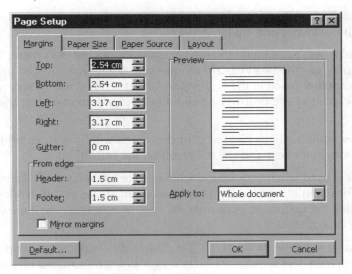

Each of these has a separate dialog box which is displayed when the appropriate tab is clicked. Many of the options in these dialog boxes are self-explanatory and the preview helps to indicate the effect of modifications.

In **Margins** two important characteristics are

- the part of the document to which the settings are to be applied

- whether facing pages need to be set with different margins, as in a book, to allow for binding.

Task 2: Printing

This tasks asks you to print the document **Letter2**.

1   With the document called **Letter2** displayed on the screen choose **File-Print Preview** to view the document in **Print Preview**.

2   Click on the   **Print**   button to call up the **Print** dialog box.

3   Click on **OK** to print the document.

Could you print this document in landscape? Try to set this up using **File-Page Setup** and selecting the **Paper Size** option. View the result on screen with **Print Preview**.

Document views

Prior to printing your document you will have viewed your document in Print Preview. Word offers several different ways of looking at your document, each of which is suitable for a different purpose. These are

■ **Normal** is the default view. Text formatting is shown, such as line spacing, font and point size, but the layout of the page is simplified

■ **Outline Layout** helps you to examine the logical structure of your document. You can choose to display just the headings. To reorganise a document you can simply drag a heading to another place in the outline, and all associated text moves with the heading. You can also raise or lower a heading's level of importance in the outline

■ **Page Layout** shows you how each page of your document will look when printed. You can edit and format the text and see the result on the screen

■ **Master Document** is used when very long documents are created which are better stored in several files than in one file. A master document allows you to work with all of the files so that the document appears to be one. Master Document view is similar to Outline Layout view

■ **Online Layout** is a new feature in Word 97. It is designed to make documents more readable on screen. Documents are increasingly being transmitted electronically and are being read directly rather than being printed. In Online Layout the text is displayed slightly larger and wraps to fit the window

■ **Print Preview** is similar to Page Layout, but displays whole pages at a reduced size and allows you to adjust various aspects of page layout, but not to edit the text.

You will probably use Normal and Page Layout most often. Normal view is useful while you get your text typed and corrected, and then Page Layout can be used to adjust the formatting and layout.

Using the **Zoom** command on the **View** menu, or the list box on the toolbar, you can reduce or magnify the display size of a document. The magnification or reduction affects only the screen display.

Task 3: Changing document views

With the document called **Letter2** on the screen, experiment with different document views, first by selecting different views from the View menu, and then by selecting Print Preview from the File menu.

Undoing mistakes

The Edit-Undo command is a valuable failsafe. Any time that you issue a command or type or delete some text, you can undo this by issuing the Edit-Undo command. This is very useful for retrieving mistakes, and moving back to a previous state. Word maintains a history of the commands you have given it and it is possible to undo a command that was not your last command.

Just to give you complete confidence, there is also the Edit-Redo command, which is displayed on the Edit menu after you have used Edit-Undo so that you can correct an undo.

Task 4: Using undo and redo

1 Open the document **Letter2** and change 'Yours faithfully' to 'Yours sincerely'.

2 Use Edit-Undo to undo the change. Try changing other words in the text of the document, and then undoing the changes.

3 Close this document and open the document **Letter2** again. Change 'Yours faithfully' to 'Yours sincerely'. Next change the date to today's date.

4 To undo both of these two changes, open the undo list box by clicking on the arrow next to the **Undo** button on the standard toolbar.

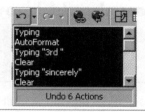

5 Select the last six actions (you may have more or fewer than this depending on what you have done) by dragging, or by pressing the down arrow key the required number of times, and pressing *Enter*.

6 Open the redo list box by clicking on the arrow next to the **Redo** button. Experiment with redoing some of the actions you have just undone. Close the document without saving changes.

Formatting text (1)

What you will learn in this unit

This unit focuses on text formatting. Modern word processors such as Word allow a great variety of formatting to be applied to text. This flexibility allows you to develop you own personal style for text presentation. At the end of this module you will be able to

- select text for revision
- use the typefonts (bold, italic etc.)
- select font (the design and size of the letters)
- alter the margins.

Formatting is used to make the text look appealing to the reader and to draw attention to headings or important points within the document.

With a powerful word processor such as Word 97 you have at your disposal many choices of typeface and typefont. Some typefaces are available in many different sizes. This is another way, in addition to the use of bold, italic and underlined type, in which to highlight or emphasise parts of your document.

What you should know already

Before you start this unit, make sure you can do the following

Skill	Covered in
Create and save a document	Unit 1
Open and edit a document	Unit 2

Selecting text

Text must be selected before its format can be changed. Text selection is also used to mark a piece of text for deletion, copying or other operations. Most of the operations described in this and later modules require text to be selected first.

Don't forget that the word processor will not change anything if you do not select the part of the document you wish to reformat first.

Any area of selected text will be highlighted. The colour of the highlight depends upon the Windows colour setting used. If the Windows default colour setting is used then the highlight is black. The various methods of selecting parts of a document are summarised in the table below.

Selection using the mouse

To select this	Do this
Word	Move the mouse cursor to the word you wish to select and double click on the left mouse button
Line	Move the mouse pointer into the left-hand edge of the screen (the pointer changes to a white, right-pointing arrow) level with the line you wish to select and click the left button
Several lines of text	Move the mouse pointer into the left-hand edge of the screen level with the first line you wish to select, click and drag downwards until the last line is selected
Sentence	Hold down the *Ctrl* key and click anywhere in the sentence
Paragraph	Move the mouse cursor into the left-hand edge level with the paragraph you wish to select and double click the left button. Alternatively, you may triple click anywhere in the paragraph
Whole document	Move the mouse cursor into the left hand edge, press the *Ctrl* key and click the left-hand mouse button or, alternatively, while the pointer is at the left edge, triple click or use **Edit-Select All**
Section of your choice	Move the mouse cursor to the beginning of the section, click the left mouse button and, while holding it down, drag the cursor to the end of the section
	Note: You may switch whole word selection on or off by customising Word (see Quick Reference 3 Customising Word)
Undoing a selection	Move the mouse pointer to anywhere in the document and click the left button
Adjusting a selection	Hold down the *Shift* key and click at the point where you wish the selection to end
	Note: If you initially selected whole units of text, e.g. lines or paragraphs, then the selection will expand or contract by these units.

Selection using the keyboard

Move the insertion point to the place in your document where you wish the selection to begin, hold down the *Shift* key and use the direction arrow keys to move the insertion point to the end of your selection.

To adjust the selection, hold down the *Shift* key and using the direction arrow keys expand or contract your selection. To cancel your selection press an arrow key without holding down the *Shift* key.

Task 1: Selecting text

Key in the following text, which is the terms of reference for a report, and save it as **Termref**.

Terms of reference

This feasibility study looks at a complete refurbishment of the multigym at Chelmer Leisure and Recreation Centre. A wide variety of equipment could be offered in a modern fitness suite. This equipment would be a vast improvement on the existing equipment. Various equipment manufacturers have been approached and three have submitted proposals for refurbishment. This report considers each of the proposals received.

The companies from which proposals have been received are:

UNIVERSAL GYM (EUROPE) LTD

ATLANTA SPORTS INDUSTRIES LTD

PHYSIQUE TRAINING EQUIPMENT LTD

Each proposal consists of a list of equipment and plans for the fitness room, plus costings. The proposals are detailed and analysed in the report. The result of the analysis of the proposals will be a recommendation for the best option.

The report will then consider how a new fitness suite would affect the centre's usage. It will also consider ways in which the new facility should be marketed.

Make the following selections and after each selection undo it.

1 Select the word feasibility.   Remember that when you have made a
                                                  successful selection, the selection will be
                                                  highlighted.

2 Select the first line in the first paragraph.

3 Select the second sentence of the second paragraph.

4 Select the last paragraph.

5 Select the whole document.

6 Select **Chelmer Leisure and Recreation Centre**. Experiment with selecting words, lines, multiple lines, paragraphs, the whole document and sections of your choice. You need to move on to the next and subsequent tasks to make use of these selections.

Using typefonts

A character may be printed in **bold** or *italic* type or <u>underlined</u>. Word offers a variety of underlining styles, as illustrated in the following table. Bold type or underlining are often used for headings to distinguish them from the rest of the text. Typefaces are also used to put emphasis on a section of text.

Type of underlining	*Effect*
Words only	<u>Underlines</u> <u>the</u> <u>words,</u> <u>not</u> <u>the</u> <u>spaces</u> <u>between</u>
Double	A double line is used as the underline
Dotted	A dotted line is used as the underline
Thick	A thick line is used as the underline
Dash	A dashed line is used as the underline
Dot dash	An alternate dot dash line is used as the underline
Dot dot dash	A dot dot dash line is used as the underline
Wave	A wavy line is used as the underline

Selection of typefonts using the mouse

As you type you can change the typefont as you go along simply by depressing the required button(s) in the formatting toolbar.

To depress a button simply move the mouse pointer to it and click. Any subsequent typing will take the typefont you have set. To switch off the typefont simply depress the button again. When a button is depressed it appears a lighter grey than the surrounding area.

To choose from the different underlining options

- use the **Format-Font** command

- in the **Font** dialog box, with the **Font** tab selected, open the **Underline:** list box, by clicking on its associated down arrow

- select the type of underlining required

- click on **OK** .

More than one typefont may be used at once, for example ***<u>bold italic double under-lined</u>*** text.

Selection of typefonts using the keyboard

Formatting may be applied using the keyboard instead of the mouse using the following key combinations.

Bold	*Ctrl/b*
Italic	*Ctrl/i*
Underline	*Ctrl/u*
Word underline	*Ctrl/Shift/w*
Double underline	*Ctrl/Shift/d*

To reformat existing text, first select the text you wish to reformat and then choose the appropriate mouse or keyboard actions.

Task 2: Applying typefonts

1   Open the document **Termref** created
    in Task 1.

2   Select the heading and make it bold   Point to the left-hand edge of the screen
    and underlined.   level with the heading and click.

3   Embolden the name of the leisure centre and put the company names in italics.
    Save the document.

Experiment by making your own selections and changing their typefont, but do not save these changes.

Task 3: Selecting typefonts

Start a new document and type in the following memo. Select the required typefont, i.e. bold, italics and underline, before keying in the text. Save as **Appmemo**.

> *the **MANCHESTER METROPOLITAN UNIVERSITY***
> ***Crewe + Alsager Faculty***
> MEMORANDUM
> TO: R. S. Symmond
> FROM: Peter Jackson
> Date: 12th Feb. 9X
> Subject: <u>Final year business project</u>
>
> When I saw you last, you suggested three possible times when we could discuss my project work. I would like to confirm that the first, *2:00pm on Monday 16th*, would suit me best and I shall see you then unless you let me know otherwise.

Using the fonts

What is a font? Word uses the word **font** to describe a typeface and its size. The typeface is the design or shape of a set of characters. Most modern ink jet and laser printers use soft fonts. These are fonts that are downloaded to the printer from the computer, such as Times New Roman and Courier New. Dot matrix printers have standard fonts such as Times Roman, Sans Serif and Courier included in their hardware. These are known as printer fonts. However, to achieve more versatility in document printing they also print soft fonts.

Word for Windows allows you to see on screen exactly what will be printed out. This is known as WYSIWYG, a mnemonic for 'What You See Is What You Get'. If you are using a dot matrix printer and you choose a printer font, Word will use a screen representation of that font. If the printer font Courier 5cpi is chosen, Word will display the text in a manner that does represent the spacing.

The font Courier is a fixed space font. This means that each character is the same width as every other character. This kind of typeface was common before the advent of sophisticated word processors where only simple formatting was available and text was lined up using spaces. Nowadays, most word processors, including Word, can take advantage of **proportionally spaced** fonts. With these, naturally wider characters, such as the letter *m*, are given more space than narrower ones, such as *j*.

A fixed space font   A proportionally spaced font

Courier   Times Roman

The font that you are using will appear in the font list box in the formatting toolbar. If you are using the standard default font it will be **Times New Roman**. On the right of this list box there is another, which contains a number. This is the point size of the characters. If you are using the default font then it will have the number **10** in it.

Choosing different fonts

Choice of font is a matter of personal taste which should be tempered by consideration for the type of document being produced. Having chosen a particular font, it is usual to use it throughout the main body of the document. Different sizes of the chosen typeface can be used for titles, headings, headers and footers. A different font from normal could be used as an alternative to draw attention to a particular portion of the text.

The font list box in the toolbar can be opened by clicking on the down arrow to the right. The box expands to show a list of the different fonts that are available. Printer fonts have a small printer symbol next to them. Some fonts have two 'Ts' next to them. These are known as True Type fonts and they are the most versatile of the screen fonts because they can be varied in size in steps of one point.

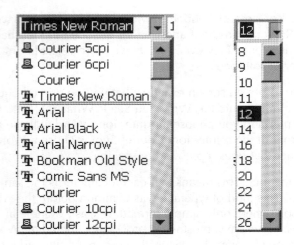

To select a font and a size for that font

■ open the font list box

■ use the scrollbar to move through the list. There are usually more fonts than can be displayed in the box. The list of fonts available to you will depend upon the type of printer you have installed

■ click on the name of your chosen font

■ open the point size list box

■ use the scrollbar to move through the list of sizes. Different fonts will have different sets of sizes available

■ click on the size required.

The font called Symbol uses the letters of the Greek alphabet; this can be useful if you are writing a scientific report. Also there is a True Type font called Wingdings which gives a variety of shapes and symbols, as shown below.

Task 4: Applying fonts

Using **Termref** created in Task 1, select each company name one at a time and apply a different font. Apply different fonts to each paragraph. Note that this creates a document that is unpleasing to read, but is a useful means of exploring the fonts available to you.

Task 5: Selecting fonts

Type in the text outlined below.

Questions of feasibility

Technical feasibility

Is the equipment available to support the project?

Operational feasibility

Will staff changes or training be necessary?

Economic feasibility

Will the benefits from the project outweigh the costs?

The first three lines are written using various sizes of the True Type font **Arial**. The next two lines are **Times New Roman**. The last two lines are **Courier**. Do not save this.

Additional font formatting

Word offers a number of additional formatting effects that can be applied through the **Format-Font** command (**Font** tab).

Effects

☐ Strikethrough ☐ Shadow ☐ Small caps
☐ Double strikethrough ☐ Outline ☐ All caps
☐ Superscript ☐ Emboss ☐ Hidden
☐ Subscript ☐ Engrave

Effect	*Appearance*
Strikethrough	A line is drawn through the text
Double strikethrough	A double line is drawn through the text
Superscript	Text is positioned in a $^{\text{raised (smaller size)}}$ position
Subscript	Text is positioned in a $_{\text{lowered (smaller size)}}$ position
Shadow	Text is shadowed
Outline	Text is outlined, best used with larger font sizes
Emboss	Text is embossed
Engrave	Text is engraved
Small caps	SMALL LETTERS ARE SHOWN IN SMALLER CAPITALS
All caps	ALL TEXT IS CAPITALISED
Hidden	Hides text. Options may be set to print hidden text but this is beyond the scope of this book

Other formatting effects include animation, which can be applied through choosing the Animation tab in the **Font** dialog box. This kind of formatting would be appropriate for a document that is to be viewed on-line, but care should be exercised so as not to overdo animation effects as the reader may find them annoying.

Controlling margins

There are three margins that you can control.

- the left margin is the position of the left edge of the text
- the right margin is the position of the right edge of the text
- the indent margin is the position of the left edge of the **first line** of a paragraph.

The positions of the edges of the text on the page can be adjusted using **File-Page Setup**. In the **Page Setup** dialog box the settings can be viewed and adjusted. There are default settings for the position of the edge of the text. For example, the default setting of the edge of the text for A4 paper is 3.17cm in from the sides. The position of the text in relation to the top and bottom of the paper may also be adjusted.

By default the left and right margins will be at the edges of the text as defined in page setup. The indent margin is at the same position as the left margin.

Adjusting the margins using the ruler

The ruler is displayed below other toolbars and is marked in centimetres (it can be altered to display inches). On the ruler there are three triangular sliders indicating the positions of the left, indent and right margins.

The left and right margin sliders are on the bottom of the ruler and the indent margin slider is on the top of the ruler.

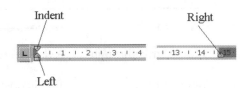

To change	Do this
Left or indent margin	Drag the appropriate margin slider to the required position on the ruler
Right margin	Drag the right triangle to the required position on the ruler

To set indents	Do this
Normal indent	Drag the indent margin so that it is to the **right** of the left margin
Hanging indent	Drag the indent margin so it is to the **left** of the left margin

Any adjustment made to the margins will affect the document at the current insertion point position and any text keyed in thereafter. Margin positions may be revised by selected the text needing revision and repositioning the margin markers.

Task 6: Controlling margins

1   With a new document open, set the left margin to 1cm and the right margin to 13cm. Type in the first paragraph of the text shown at the end of this task.

2   Set the left margin to 2cm, the indent margin to 3cm and the right margin to 12cm before keying in the second paragraph.

3   The margins for the third paragraph are at left and indent 3cm, right 10cm.

4   Save this document as **Qdesign**.

> Questionnaires provide a structured and formal way in which information may be collected.
>
> The advantages of questionnaires are that they are relatively inexpensive, they are free from interviewer distortion and if the response is anonymous, personal or controversial questions may be asked.
>
> The disadvantages of questionnaires are that there may be a low response, questions usually have to be simple and straightforward and if they are anonymous then there is no information about the person who has answered them.

Changing existing margins

The margins of existing text can be altered by selecting that text and then adjusting the margin positions. If you alter the position of the margins when no text is selected then your alterations will only affect the paragraph that the insertion point is currently in.

Adjusting the margins using the menu

The margins may be altered using Format-Paragraph. Select the Indents and Spacing tab in the Paragraph dialog box and alter the values shown in the Indentation section.

In this section there are three boxes, Left:, Right: and Special:. The number in each associated box may be altered to position the margins. The Special: list box allows the type of indenting to be chosen.

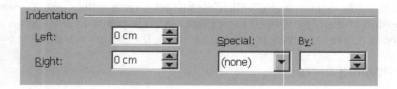

Task 7: Altering margins

Open **Termref** and change the position of the left margin of the three company name paragraphs.

1 Select all three paragraphs and drag the left and then the indent margin right by 2cm.

2 Select the first paragraph and drag the indent margin right by 1cm. Save the document.

3 Experiment by selecting other portions of the document and altering the left, right and indent margins, but do not save these changes.

Adjusting the left margin using the buttons

Word provides a quick way to adjust the left margin by means of two buttons on the

formatting tool bar.

The button on the right moves the left margin in to the right by half an inch (1.27cm) and the button on the left moves the left margin out to the left by half an inch.

Task 8: A private advertisement

Create an advertisement for a student notice board. Type the following advertisement.

> For Sale - One pair of Ladies Ice Skates, size 6. In very good condition as only used one winter. £15 o.n.o.
>
> Contact Louise Green Room C27 Derby Hall

To make it stand out typefonts could be used.

> **For Sale** - One pair of *Ladies Ice Skates, size 6*. In <u>very good condition</u> as only used one winter. £15 o.n.o.
>
> Contact **Louise Green** Room C27 Derby Hall

Different fonts could be used to make it more eye-catching.

> **For Sale** - One pair of ***Ladies Ice Skates, size 6***. In <u>very good condition</u> as only used one winter. £15 o.n.o.
>
> Contact Louise Green Room C27 Derby Hall

The last line could be separated from the first paragraph by adjusting the amount of space before it. The first paragraph could have a hanging indent set, producing the following effect.

> **For Sale** - One pair of ***Ladies Ice Skates, size 6***. In <u>very good condition</u> as only used one winter. **£15 o.n.o.**
>
> Contact Louise Green *Room C27* Derby Hall

Formatting text (2)

What you will learn in this unit

This unit continues the theme of text formatting developed in Unit 3. At the end of this unit you will be able to

- create a hanging indent
- use bullets and point numbers
- change the alignment of text
- alter the spacing between lines and characters.

It is worth the effort of practising the creation of indents as this can enable you to produce documents where the text lines up correctly. The aim of text formatting is to produce a professional and pleasing document.

What you should know already

Before you start this unit, make sure you can do the following.

Skill	Covered in
Create and save a document	Unit 1
Open and edit a document	Unit 2
Select text, apply fonts, control margins	Unit 3

Hanging indent

This is where the left and indent margins are set up so that the left margin is to the right of the indent margin. Hanging indents are commonly used where a list of points is being made and the first words of a paragraph need to stand out.

Previous Paragraph
Sample TextSample TextSample TextSample TextSample TextSample
    TextSample TextSample TextSample TextSample TextSample
    TextSample TextSample TextSample TextSample TextSample
    TextSample TextSample TextSample TextSample Text
Following Paragraph Following Paragraph Following Paragraph Following Paragraph Follow

Task 1: Setting a hanging indent

To create the following example

CHELMER LEISURE AND RECREATION CENTRE

AEROBICS OPEN DAY

Step　　One of the best ways to start your fitness programme. Our fitness demonstrators will be on hand to advise you on a suitable fitness programme.

Cycle　　Tone up those flabby thighs and strengthen those backs. Our cycles simulate real cycling conditions, which can be individually tailored to your fitness programme.

Row　　Fancy yourself in the boat race? Try your hand at our computer controlled rowing machine.

1　Use a new document, type in the two lines of the heading (try to reproduce the font) and press *Enter*.

2　Drag the left margin to the right 4cm.

3　Key in the type of activity using the font Arial, bold and size 14.

4　After keying in the activity name press the *Tab* key to tab the insertion point to line up with the left margin.

5　Enter the rest of the text comprising the activity; it will word wrap around onto the left margin. Use a different typeface such as Courier New, font size 10.

6　Press *Enter* for a new line.

7　Repeat steps 3-6 for each aerobic activity.

8　Save this document as **Openday**.

Bullets and numbered points

To distinguish a list of points from the rest of the text it is usual to highlight them using bullets or point numbers. A bullet is a symbol at the start of each point as shown below.

FINDINGS FROM MARKET RESEARCH

Information has been collated from the returned questionnaires resulting in

- a consensus of opinion that present facilities are inadequate and that attendance is poor

- the numbers of users, particularly female, would increase if the facility was refurbished

- the majority of users are car owners, so promotion in a wider area could attract new clients

- nearly two thirds of the people surveyed had never used the existing multi-gym

- aerobic activities were popular

- entertainment, such as satellite television, would be an attraction in the new fitness suite

---

Hanging indents, as described above, are used when the text comprises a set of points. Word offers two buttons on the formatting toolbar, which will help you to type a numbered or bulleted list.

Task 2: Numbered points

Five Fab Top Tips to Reduce Fat in Your Diet.

1 Fry less often. Grill, bake, nuke in the microwave or boil instead.

2 Trim visible fat off meat, don't eat the skin on chicken, skim fat off casseroles and buy lean cuts.

3 Cut down on chocolate, cakes, pastries and biscuits.

4 Use less cooking oil or fat, less salad oil, less mayonnaise and other sauces.

5 Be aware of the high fat content of some foods perceived as 'healthy' such as peanuts, avocado, polyunsaturated margarine and oils and 'low fat' spreads.

To create this example

1 Start a new document, key in the heading line and create a new line using *Enter*.

2 Click on the point numbering icon. A number appears and the insertion point will be positioned on the left margin. Notice how the left and indent margins are set.

3 Type in the text for the point, press *Enter* and click. The next number is automatically incremented.

4 When you have finished the list press *Enter* and click on the **Numbering** button to stop automatic numbering and reset the indent margin. Save this document as **Fattips**.

Task 3: Bullet points

Start a new document and create the Findings from Market Research list (used above as an illustration).

1   Type in the heading and first sentence and create a new line using *Enter*.

2   Click on the **Bullets** button. A bullet will appear and the insertion point will be ready positioned on the left margin. Notice how the left and indent margins are set.

3   Key in the text for that point.

4   Make a new line, to automatically create the bullet for the next point. Repeat for each point. After the last point press *Enter* and switch off the bulleting by clicking on the **Bullets** button. Save this document as **Findings**.

Customising bullets and numbers

When you click on the **Numbering** or **Bullets** button Word will apply the default numbering or bulleting to your document. You may customise this using **Format-Bullets and Numbering**. The **Bullets and Numbering** dialog box offers a choice of different styles of bullets under the **Bulleted** tab and different styles of numbering under the **Numbering** tab. Click on the style you want and click on **OK**.

To alter the font of a point number then select the paragraph mark at the end of the point (click on the **Show/Hide ¶** button to display them) and apply the formatting you require.

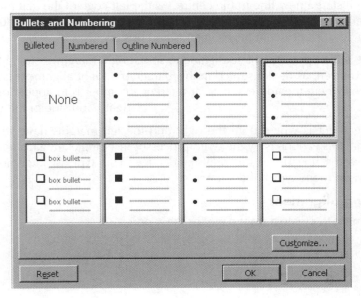

Task 4: Customising bullet points

In this task the bullets in the document **Findings** will be modified.

1 Highlight the bulleted paragraphs in this document.

2 Choose **Format-Bullets and Numbering**.

3 Select a different bullet from those presented by clicking on it and click on **OK**.

4 Save the document as **Findings**.

Text alignment

Alignment is the way in which the text appears between the left and right margins. In Word there are four types of alignment: left, right, centre and full justification. Depressing the appropriate button on the formatting toolbar can alter the type of alignment.

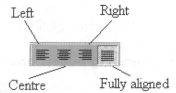

Left alignment causes the text to have a straight left margin and an uneven right margin. The uneven right margin is caused because there is a standard space between each word and each character has a specified amount of space associated with it. If a word does not fit at the end of the line then it is wrapped around onto the next line. This paragraph is written using left alignment.

Centre alignment causes each line of a paragraph to be positioned centrally between the left and right margins. If you use centre alignment while typing, the insertion point will start a new line in the centre. As the left edge of the text moves to the left the insertion point moves to the right. This type of alignment is very useful for titles, title pages, menus and posters.

Right alignment is the opposite of left alignment, so the right margin is straight and the left margin is uneven, as demonstrated in this paragraph. Right alignment is used in letters or memos where the address, date or reference number is to appear on the right-hand side of the page.

Fully justified alignment is where both the right and the left margins have straight edges. The way that this is done is by the word processor inserting extra gaps into the line so that the words line up at the right-hand edge. This type of alignment is commonly chosen for many types of documents.

Task 5: Selecting alignment

Start a new document to create a front page for the report.

the Manchester Metropolitan University
Crewe + Alsager Faculty

Environment & Enterprise Project
**The Refurbishment of the Multi-Gym into a
Fitness Suite
at Chelmer Leisure and Recreation Centre
A Feasibility Study**

By: Sarah Leveridge
Tutor: R. S. Symmond
Course: HND Business and Finance
Date: 1st February 1996

1 Select Arial point size 15 for the name of the institution.

2 For the title, select centre alignment by clicking on the appropriate icon.

3 Key in the words Environment & Enterprise Project using Times New Roman, bold, italic, 15pts. Press *Enter*.

4 For the main title use Times New Roman, bold, 16pts.

5 Select right alignment.

6 Using Arial, italic, 14pts, key in the author, tutor, course and date.

7 Save this document as **Front**.

Line spacing

Line spacing refers to the space between the bottom of one line and the bottom of the next line. Normally text is typed in 'single spacing', i.e. line spacing is one. Word automatically adjusts the line height to accommodate the size of the font you are using.

Choose **Format-Paragraph** to alter the line spacing in the document.

Three types of spacing that are most commonly used are

- Single: single spacing that Word can increase depending on the size of font used
- 1.5 lines: one-and-a-half line spacing that Word can increase
- Double: double spacing that Word can increase.

Task 6: Selecting line spacing

Into a new document enter the text outlined below.

SUMMARY

Chelmer Leisure Centre is one of the facilities of Cheshire Leisure Services. The existing multi-gym facility has had little money spent on it over the past few years and has experienced a decrease in the number of users. Market research shows that there is a need for this particular facility to be updated.

Three manufacturers of fitness equipment have put forward proposals for the refurbishment of the multi-gym into a fitness suite. The proposal chosen is from Atlanta Sports Industries Ltd. The overall cost for refurbishment will be £21,000.

---

1 Using **Format-Paragraph**, choose one-and-a-half spacing and key in the first paragraph.

2 Using **Format-Paragraph** again, select double spacing before keying in the second paragraph.

3 Save this document as **Summary**.

Character spacing

There is another form of spacing that can be used and that is spacing between characters. By choosing **Format-Font**, and clicking on the Character Spacing tab the Spacing: list box may be opened to show the list of spacing choices.

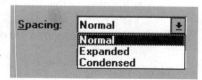

Task 7: Selecting character spacing

Key in the sentence shown below following these instructions.

1 Choose **Format-Font** and click on the **Character Spacing** tab.

2 Open the Spacing: box, select Expanded and key in the first half of the text up to the word 'and'.

3   Change to Normal spacing using **Format-Font** and type 'and'.

4   Change to condensed spacing and key in the rest of the sentence.

> Expanded   spacing   will   put   more   space   in   between   the letters andcondensedspacingwillreducetheamountofspacingbetweenletters.

Task 8: A business advertisement

The following advertisement was created using the fonts Arial and Wingdings. All of the text is centre aligned.

TOP-HOLE INSURANCE

BROKERS LIMITED

FOR ALL YOUR

INSURANCE REQUIREMENTS

 **LOOK**

NO FURTHER

WE CAN INSURE YOUR HOUSEHOLD

CONTENT UP TO £50,000 FOR UNDER

£1.50 PER WEEK

MOTOR INSURANCE

OVER 25 AND NO PREVIOUS INSURANCE?

If you have held a Full Driving Licence for 4 years with no accidents or convictions

THIRD PARTY - from only £100

FULLY COMPREHENSIVE - from only £150

Call us on (0123) 456789 *NOW!*

A variety of point sizes are used. Try point size 18 for the first two lines. Try point size 21, bold for the next two lines.

There is space above the word 'look'. Use paragraph spacing to adjust this. The hands are created using Wingdings, characters F and E, at a point size of 44. There is an easier way to find the Wingdings characters (or characters from any other font) and that is to use **Insert-Symbol** and select the symbol you require from the matrix of symbols presented. To see characters available with other fonts open the font list box and select the font desired.

Try a point size of 35 for 'look', which is bold and italic.

See if you can create the rest of the advertisement. Consider the typeface, the point size, the space before (or after a paragraph) and the character spacing of each line.

Task 9: A poster

Create the poster shown below.

1   Set the left and right margins to 1cm and 13cm respectively.

2   Choose a suitably sized font and centre align the title.

3   Set a hanging indent for the question and answer. Move the left margin to 2.5cm. Key in the question and answer text.

4   Put the left margin back to 1cm. Key in the paragraph of text.

5   Use centre alignment for the last section.

6   Check that you have used bold and italics where shown. Save the document as **Poster**, preview and print.

Introducing the
New Generation Bodywrap System

Q.   How does it work?

A.   The Quickslim method of bodywrapping does not depend upon fluid loss through perspiration, but on osmotic activity reducing the inter-cellular fluid.

A course of Quickslim treatment is especially effective when combined with a G5 treatment and a sensible diet.

See the difference for yourself!

One Wrap £38 - a 90 minute treatment

Discounts available on courses

Contact: Mary at '*The Beauty Room*'

Copying formats

If you apply some formatting to a section of your text and wish to apply exactly the same formatting to another section of your text then you can use the Format Painter facility. To copy paragraph and character formatting

■ select the text that has the formatting you want to copy

■ click on the **Format Painter** button in the standard toolbar

■ select the text to which you'd like to apply the formatting.

If you wish to copy formatting to several locations then double-click on the **Format Painter** button. Select each portion of text in turn and when you have finished click once on the **Format Painter** button.

Task 10: Painting formats

1 Select Times New Roman, point size 12 and key in the following text but without the formatting shown in the example.

Serif and sans serif fonts

A font is a particular design of type, which comes in a variety of styles (plain, bold, italics etc.) and a variety of sizes. Many fonts have special purposes and a typeface which works well as a header may be very hard to read if used as body text. Arial is a sans *serif* typeface, Times New Roman is a *serif* face. *Serif* are the little tails on the tips of the characters' horizontal and vertical strokes. They help to make *serif* faces look dignified, solid and unhurried.

Sans *serif* (and sans means without) types are designed to be bold and easy to read, and economical with space on the paper. Sans *serif* is often used for hard information, such as instructions. It is common to have sans *serif* headlines and serif body text - *The* Guardian newspaper uses a combination of both to make up its masthead (*title*).

Type size

This is usually measured in points, with 72 points to the inch. But because character width, kerning (space between the letters) and leading (space between the lines) depend upon how the type has been designed, type in one font point size (typically 10) rarely covers the same area as the same point size in a different font. This can make layout much more complicated.

---

2 Select the first heading and change it to Arial, 12pts, bold.

---

3 Select this heading and click on the **Format Painter** button. Select the second heading and when you release the mouse button you will see the format applied.

---

4 Select one of the words 'serif' and make it Arial, italic.

---

5 While it is still selected double click on the **Format Painter** button. Now select each word 'serif' in turn. When you have finished click once on the Format Painter button.

---

6 Apply the formatting to '*The* Guardian' and save the document as **Font**.

Improving your documents

What you will learn in this unit

This unit introduces some activities that will aid document production and presentation. These activities include

■ moving and copying text

■ deleting text

■ moving quickly around a document

■ finding and replacing text.

Presentation has an important effect on the reader's initial reactions. When you are producing a document, whether it be for your customers, managers or tutors, good presentation will predispose them to view the document favourably. It is important to proofread your work and make amendments, if necessary, using the techniques introduced in this unit.

What you should know already

Before you start this unit, make sure you can do the following.

Skill	Covered in
Create and save a document	Unit 1
Open and edit a document	Unit 2
Select text	Unit 3

Moving, copying and deleting text

When a document is being written it is easy to use the word processor to make revisions. Revisions can range from restructuring a sentence to rearranging the order in which paragraphs appear. The word processor's abilities to move, copy and delete text are an invaluable aid to putting thoughts onto 'electronic' paper.

Moving: cutting and pasting

If a section of the document is out of place, be it a few words, sentences or paragraphs, then it can easily be moved to the right place. First select the section to be moved and use **Edit-Cut**, or alternatively click on the **Cut** button in the standard toolbar.

The selection will disappear from the screen. It is stored in a temporary area in the computer's memory called the clipboard. It is important to remember that this is only temporary storage and if anything else is copied to the clipboard then the new overwrites the old. To avoid losing the contents of the clipboard an **Edit-Cut** operation should be followed by an **Edit-Paste** operation as soon as possible.

To insert the information from the clipboard into the document, first position the insertion point at the correct place within the document and use **Edit-Paste** or click on the **Paste** button in the standard toolbar.

Task 1: Moving: cut and paste

With a new document open type in the following sentence.

> The local government environment is changing fast with new laws and new standards appearing almost every month.

1 Select the portion 'with new laws and new standards appearing almost every month'.

2 Using **Edit-Cut** will remove this portion and place it on the clipboard.

3 Move the insertion point to the beginning of the sentence and use **Edit-Paste**.

4 Tidy up the sentence so that it now reads

> With new laws and new standards appearing almost every month the local government environment is changing fast.

Task 2: Moving: drag and drop

This is a method of moving which is ideally suited to small selections and small movements, for example, rewording a sentence. First select the section to be moved and then click on the selection and hold down the mouse button. As the pointer is dragged notice that at the bottom of the arrow is a small grey rectangle and also a small grey insertion point which follows the pointer movements. This insertion point is the position at which the selection will be dropped when the mouse button is released.

Type in the following sentence:

> If you wish to reserve a place complete and return the reply slip overleaf please.

1 Highlight the word 'please' and the space before it.

2 Drag the insertion marker to the end of 'place'.

3 Release the button and the sentence should read

If you wish to reserve a place please complete and return the reply slip overleaf.

Copying and pasting

This is very similar to cut and paste except that the selected text remains in the document and a copy of it is placed on the clipboard. The copy that is in the clipboard is available to be pasted into the document.

First select the section to be copied and use **Edit-Copy** or click on the **Copy** button in the toolbar. Position the insertion point at the place in the document where the copy is to go and use **Edit-Paste** or click on the **Paste** button. The contents of the clipboard may be pasted into the document as many times as required.

Deleting

Normal deleting as a running correction can be achieved using either the *Backspace* or the *Delete* key. However, if a larger portion of the document needs to be deleted then it may be selected and then removed by pressing the *Delete* key.

Undoing

Remember that in any of the above activities if the desired change does not occur use **Edit-Undo** straight away and try again. **Edit-Undo** will undo your last action. Alternatively, click on the **Undo** button. If you wish to undo more than one action use the undo drop-down list.

Task 3: Copy and paste

Start a new document and key in the following text. Save it as **Centre**.

INTRODUCTION

The Chelmer Leisure and Recreation Centre is at present a very basic gym. It is used by people from a wide range of socio-economic backgrounds. The majority of people using the centre come from the surrounding catchment area.

It is proposed to apply for Local Council funding for refurbishing the present multi-gym facility into a fitness suite. In recent years little money has been spent on the multi-gym. This has resulted in a decrease in the number of users. Present users of the multi-gym are weightlifters most of whom are male.

The fitness centre offers a wide range of activities. The centre is also an extremely popular venue for aerobics, step classes, keep fit and popmobility. These classes are responsible for attracting a large number of female users to the centre, who, in the event of refurbishment of the multi-gym, would be a large target group. The aerobic based activities account for nearly half of the total number of users of the centre. It is hoped that with the introduction of a fitness suite, those existing users will also use the new facility.

Using **Edit-Cut** and **Edit-Paste** reword the first sentence of the last paragraph to read 'A wide range of activities is offered by the fitness centre'.

1   First select the part of the sentence 'a wide range of activities' and use **Edit-Cut**.

2   Move the insertion point to the beginning of the sentence and use **Edit-Paste**.

3   The sentence requires some tidying up. Make the first word a capital A. An alternative way in which to change the case of a word is to select it and press *Shift/F3*.

4   Put a space after 'activities' and type the word 'is'.

5   Select the word 'offers', use **Edit-Cut**, position the insertion point after 'is', use **Edit-Paste** and change 'offers' to 'offered by'.

6   Make the 'T' in 'The' lower case and remove the space before the full stop.

7   Reword the fourth sentence to read 'Nearly half of the total number of users of the centre take part in aerobic based activities'. Save the amended document.

Moving quickly around a document

Normally you move around a document by moving the insertion point. The insertion point can be moved using the *arrow* keys or by moving the mouse pointer to a certain point and clicking. There are also a number of ways to move quickly to another part of the document. These are summarised in the table below.

Key combination	Result
Home	Moves insertion point to the start of the current line.
End	Moves insertion point to the end of the current line.
Page Up and *Page Down*	Move either up or down by one screen height. The insertion point generally remains in the same position on the screen, however, it is in a different part of the document.
Ctrl/Home	Moves the insertion point to the beginning of the document.
Ctrl/End	Moves the insertion point to the end of the document.
Ctrl/Page Up	Moves the insertion point to the top of the current page.

Ctrl/Page Down	Moves the insertion point to the top of the following page.
Ctrl/←	Moves the insertion point to the beginning of the current word.
Ctrl/→	Moves the insertion point to the beginning of the next word.
Ctrl/g **(Edit-go to)**	Moves to a particular page in the document. Enter the required page number into the dialog box.

Using the scrollbars

There are scrollbars to the right and the bottom of the document window. Using the scrollbars will allow up, down, left or right movement around the document.

By clicking on the box with an arrow at either end of the scrollbar a small movement in the direction of the arrow will be made. By dragging the scroll box to another position in the scrollbar larger movements can be made. Clicking in the vertical scrollbar has the effect of *Page Up* or *Page Down* depending which side of the scroll box you click. Clicking in the horizontal scrollbar causes movements of a screen width. Note that when scrolling the insertion point remains static.

The two double-headed arrow buttons on the vertical scrollbar will move you to either the previous or next page. The **Select Browse Object** button allows you to move through your document, using the double-headed arrow buttons, stopping at particular objects, for example, headings or tables. However, as we are considering simple documents we will consider the use of this button later.

Finding and replacing text

The ability to search through a document and find a particular section of text, or 'string', and if required replace it with another, is an extremely useful feature. There are varied uses for **Find** and **Find and Replace**. An example for each follows.

By using **Find and Replace** a mistake such as an incorrectly spelt company name can be corrected throughout a document. **Find** is useful in proofreading. For example, finding a topic name such as 'fitness centre' will enable all parts of the document that deal with aspects of this topic to be found. This helps to ensure consistency throughout a document.

Find and replace

Finding and replacing allows a particular string to be located and replaced by an alternative string. **Edit-Replace** is used to invoke the replace facility and the **Find and Replace** dialog box appears with the **Replace** tab selected.

In the **Find what:** box enter the text string to be located. This text string may be part of a word, a whole word or several words. The **Find what:** list box may be opened to list the previous four searches that you may have made and you may select from one of these. In the **Replace with:** box enter the replacement string.

To see more options for replacing click on the ▐More▌ button, which expands the dialog box. Replacing works for all of the document, from the insertion point to the beginning or from the insertion point to the end, depending upon whether, All, Up or Down is selected in the **Search:** box.

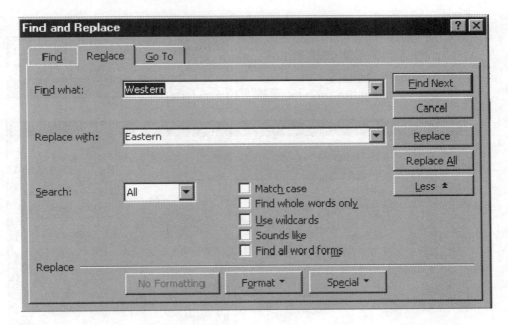

If the search string being used is a single word which could also form part of a larger word then the '**Find whole words only**' option may be selected. If the aim is to find all of the whole words and any words that contain the search string then leave the check box blank. Click on this option to put a cross in the check box if the aim is only to find the whole word.

Normal searching is not case sensitive so searching for the string '**the**' will find 'the', 'The', 'THE' etc. and any words containing 'the', 'The' and 'THE'. To make the search case sensitive click on the '**Match case**' option.

Find and **Replace** will use the text in the **Find what** box to search for any character or string as part of a word. To only search for whole words for example, **place** and by ticking **Find whole words only** will find only find place, not words such as replace and placement where place forms part of the word.

Once the search string has been found there are three replacement options available.

■ To replace the search string with the replace string click on the ▐**Replace**▌ button.

- To skip to the next occurrence of the search string without replacing it click on the **Find Next** button.

- To replace all occurrences of the search string with the replace string click on **Replace All** .

Note: The **Replace All** option should be used with the utmost caution. Unintentional replacements may occur, especially if the search string forms part of other words.

Find

To search for a particular string choose **Edit-Find** or click on the **Select Browse Object** button in the scrollbar and click on the **Find** icon. This will produce the **Find and Replace** dialog box with the **Find** tab selected.

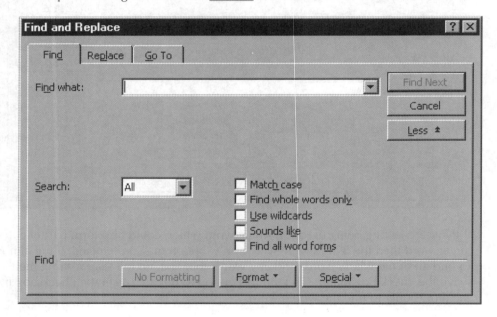

In the **Find what:** box enter the text string to be located. Press *Enter* and then click on the **Find Next** button to find the next occurrence of the specified string. To find the next occurrence click on the **Find Next** button again. The direction of the search may be controlled by the choice of **Search:** option.

Task 4: Find and replace

Into a new document, key in the following text. Save this document as **Usage**.

> **Usage of the centre**
>
> Chelmer Leisure Centre is a fairly small centre which offers no 'wet' sporting activities. The centre does not have sauna or solarium facilities. Approximately a mile away there is a swimming pool which offers these facilities.
>
> The centre is well used. In a recent eight month period over 26 thousand people passed through the centre. On average over three thousand people per month are using the facilities offered by the centre. This gives an average daily figure of over 100 people. However, demand fluctuates depending on the day of the week and whether it was a holiday period.
>
> Popular activities offered by the centre are Step, Popmobility, Keep fit and Aerobics. The figures for people attending these over the eight month period studied are Step 5058, Popmobility 4779, Keep Fit 679 and Aerobics 2080.
>
> The total number of people attending these activities account for nearly half the total number of people using the Leisure centre over the eight month period studied.

To use the Replace facility

1 Position the insertion point at the beginning of the first paragraph.

2 Use **Edit-Replace**; in the **Find what:** box type 'people' and in the **Replace with:** box type 'clients'.

3 Click on **Find Next** and use **Replace** . The word 'people' will be replaced by 'clients' and Word will find the next occurrence of 'people'.

4 Repeat the **Replace** command to replace all occurrences of 'people' with 'clients'.

5 Reposition the insertion point at the beginning of the first paragraph.

6 Use **Edit-Replace**; in the **Find what:** box type 'studied' and in the **Replace with:** box type 'analysed'.

7 Click on **Find Next** and skip the first occurrence using **Find Next** . This time use the **Replace** command to replace the remaining occurrences of 'studied' with 'analysed'.

Extra features in finding and replacing

In both the **Find** and the **Replace** dialog boxes there is a **Format** button. This allows a search string to be defined very specifically in terms of its font, colour and the formatting applied to it.

For example, it is possible to search for the word 'text' where the font is Times New Roman, size 14 and colour green and where it appears in a paragraph that is centre justified.

Finding and replacing special characters

Word allows for many special characters to be located and replaced. A special character is one that usually has an invisible effect upon the document. Examples of special characters include the tab character, the paragraph mark and the page break. Special characters can be made to show by clicking on the **Show/Hide ¶**

¶ button. Clicking this button again will cause them to disappear.

For example, suppose a piece of text is imported into Word, which was originally created by another word processor. At the end of every line regardless of whether it is the end of a sentence or paragraph there is a new line character. In Word a new line character or paragraph mark is only necessary at the end of paragraphs.

To allow Word to perform word wrapping on this piece of text the superfluous paragraph marks will need to be removed. Some will be kept; that is, those that mark the end of each paragraph.

This task can be performed by using **Edit-Replace**. Click on the **Special** button and select Paragraph Mark from the list. ^**p** appears in the **Find what:** box. Enter a space in the **Replace with**: box. Click on the **Replace** button where a replacement is required and the **Find Next** button where a replacement is not required, i.e. where there are ends of paragraphs.

Some of the special characters you may wish to find or replace are tab (^**t**) characters and non-automatic (or hard) page breaks (^**m**).

Task 5: Displaying special character marks

Open the document **Usage** from the Task 4 and click on the **Show/Hide ¶** button. If you have a paragraph marker at the end of every line you have not been using word wrap properly. Read Unit 1 again. Note which other special characters are displayed. Click on the **Show/Hide ¶** button to remove the special characters from the display.

Task 6: Find and replace

Type the following paragraph into a new document.

The mouse is a hand-held device connected to a computer, which can be used as an alternative to the keyboard for issuing commands or instructions. Its shape resembles a mouse with a cable for a tail and buttons for eyes. Unlike a real mouse the cable emerges from between the eyes! The operator's hand grips the mouse between thumb and little finger allowing the first and second fingers to rest over the buttons.

Sliding the mouse over the desktop, ideally using a mouse mat, beside the computer, rotates a direction sensitive ball inside, which in turn causes a pointer to move around the screen.

Commands are chosen from an on-screen menu by pointing to them with the tip of the pointer and usually 'clicking' the left-hand button.

In painting applications the pointer can be used as a drawing tool such as a paintbrush. On a colour monitor a palette of colours is available and selecting from the palette puts paint on the paintbrush. It is usual to be able to alter the thickness of the line painted by the paintbrush. There may also be an air-brush tool which creates a spray painting effect.

1   Position the insertion point at the top of the document.

2   Using **Edit-Find** and searching down through the text, find every instance of the word 'paint'.

3   Position the insertion point at the end of the document

4   Use **Edit-Find** to find the word 'mouse', searching up through the text.

5   Repeat the search to find every instance of the whole word 'paint'.

6   Using **Edit-Replace**, change the word 'mouse' to 'rodent'.

Improving text

What you will learn in this unit

This unit follows on from the previous one, with more tasks that will aid document presentation. These activities include

■ checking spelling and using AutoCorrect

■ making AutoText entries

■ using the thesaurus

■ using the grammar checker.

There are various ways in which the word processor can help to improve the text in a document. Many word processor users are not trained typists and are prone to make errors while keying in their work. Word will check your work as you key it in. Mistakes are shown with a wiggly line underneath so that you can instantly revise them by clicking on the word with the *right* mouse button, which generates a short-cut menu. The spell check facility will provide suggestions for the correct spelling if you are not sure. Even so, it is good practice to check your document for spelling and grammatical mistakes before printing the final copy. The word processor cannot proofread a document so after checking the spelling and grammar always proofread your work. If the work would benefit from rewording use the thesaurus to help.

Checking spelling and grammar as you work

You will already have noticed Word's ability to check your spelling and grammar as you type. Spelling errors are underlined with a red wavy line and grammatical errors with a green wavy line. Transposing letters while typing often causes a spelling mistake, and a typing error such as this can easily be amended. However, there will be a number of occasions when Word will not recognise a word because it is not in its dictionary, as illustrated below.

wiggly

Where a spelling error is marked, point to the word and click the **right** mouse button. This displays a shortcut menu, which will suggest alternatives, allow you to ignore all occurrences of the word, add the word to the dictionary or start the spell checker, as described later in this unit.

Where a grammatical error is marked, point to any of the underlined words and click the **right** mouse button. This displays a shortcut menu that will suggest alternatives, allow you to ignore the error, or start the grammar checker, as described later in this unit.

Task 1: Correcting spelling as you work

In a new document experiment by keying in deliberately misspelt words and point to these words. Click on the right mouse button to see the shortcut menu. Just use the suggestions and Ignore All; do not add any words to the dictionary or start the spell checker. Close the document without saving it.

Using the spelling and grammar checker

The spell checker can be used to check a selection or the whole document. If a selection is to be checked, select it first. Use **Tools-Spelling and Grammar**, click on the ▐ **Spelling and Grammar** ▌ button, use the shortcut key *F7* or choose Spelling from the shortcut menu. If you have not made a selection Word will start the spell check from the position of the insertion point.

The **Spelling and Grammar** dialog box appears.

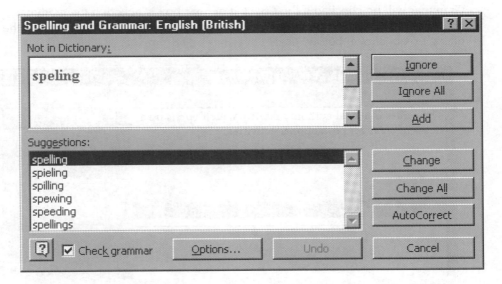

Both spelling and grammar are checked, but if you only wish to check the spelling then remove the tick from the **Check grammar** box.

When the spell checker comes across a word it does not recognise it shows it in the **Not in Dictionary:** box. In the **Suggestions:** box the spell checker offers a correction, or a list of possible corrections. Behind the spelling dialog box the document can be seen with the word in question highlighted.

There are a number of options available, shown by the buttons.

- If the correct spelling is in the **Suggestions** box click to highlight it and click on the ▐ **Change** ▌ button.

- If you think that the mistake may be repeated throughout the document then use the ▐ **Change All** ▌ button instead of the ▐ **Change** ▌ button.

- If the word is correct but is not in the spell checker's dictionary then choose **Ignore** or you may **Add** the word to the dictionary. Consult the Office Assistant for information about adding to or creating your own dictionary. Use **Ignore All** to ignore all occurrences of the word throughout the document.

- If you want Word to automatically correct the mistake if you make it again while typing then click on the **AutoCorrect** button. AutoCorrect is discussed in more detail in the following section.

- You can customise the spelling and grammatical rules used for checking by clicking on the **Options** button.

If a selection is not made, the spell checker will check the entire document, and when finished will return to the original place of the insertion point. If you are checking a selection, when that is finished you have the option to carry on and check the whole document.

Grammar will be checked if the **Check grammar** box is ticked. If the grammar checker finds a sentence with questionable grammar or style, it displays it in the dialog box as shown below.

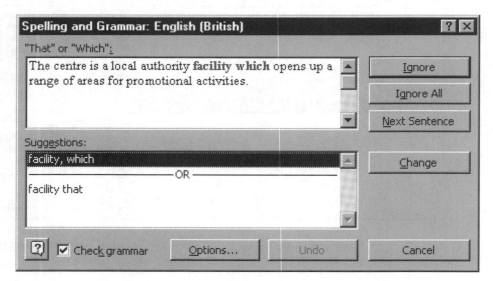

Words related to the suspected error are displayed in coloured (default green) type. The grammar checker displays suggested corrections in the **Suggestions:** box. Choices of action are

- make a suggested correction. Select one of the corrections from the **Suggestions:** box and click on the **Change** button

- make your own corrections in the document. Make the document window active by clicking on it. Edit the sentence and click on the **Resume** button in the dialog box to resume checking the document

- ignore the questioned word or sentence without making changes. Click on the **Ignore** button

- ignore all occurrences of this error in the document. Click on the **Ignore All** button

- skip the entire sentence. Click on the **Next Sentence** button to start checking the next sentence.

Task 2: Correcting grammar as you work

The following piece of text is deliberately incorrect. Key it into a new document exactly. As each mistake is highlighted, point and click with the right mouse button and correct the text. You should find **'Atlanta**'s' suggested for '**Atlantas**', '**it's**' for '**its**' and '**There**' for '**Their**'.

> Atlantas proposal was the one considered the most attractive for Chelmer Leisure and Recreation Centre. The Athena equipment offers a great advantage due to the nature of it's design. There equipment is designed so that it can be positioned 'back to back' to save valuable space.

Task 3: Checking a document for spelling and grammatical errors

The following piece of text is also deliberately incorrect. Key it into the document you used for the last task. Note that the word 'colour' is deliberately spelt the American way and will be highlighted if the English (British) dictionary is being used. To check which dictionary is in use, choose **Tools-Language-Set Language**. If English (British) is not being used then select the whole document and set English (British) using **Tools-Language-Set Language**. If this is a problem check your Regional Settings in the Windows 95 Control Panel.

Correct the piece as you see fit, you may either accept changes or try rewording the piece. It is not necessary to save this.

> Plastic credit cards would be issued to the members, one color indicating full and another to indicate concessionary members. These would be signed by the user and handed in at the reception by the member while they use the facility. Each card would be printed with the details of the membership and times for the use by the member. Each occasion a member uses the facility it would be recorded by the receptionist, to monitor usage of the scheme.

AutoCorrect

You can tell Word about your common typing mistakes so that as you type Word will monitor your typing for these mistakes and automatically correct them. Word maintains a list of common 'mistypes' and their corrections and Word will correct you, if you mistype a word from this list. For example the word 'occurrance' would be corrected as 'occurrence'. If you do not wish Word to do this then you can switch off this feature using **Tools-AutoCorrect** and remove the cross from the **Replace text as you type** check box.

You may add 'mistype' words and their corrections to the AutoCorrect list, either through using **Tools-AutoCorrect** or by clicking on the ▏**AutoCorrect**▕ button in the **Spelling** dialog box.

The **AutoCorrect** dialog box also offers the following corrections, which you may switch on or off by either ticking the appropriate check box or leaving it blank.

■ Correction of two capitals at the beginning of a word (may happen if you type quickly and do not release the *Shift* key soon enough).

■ Capitalisation of the first word of a sentence.

■ Capitalisation of the names of the days of the week.

■ Correction of typing when *Caps Lock* has been left on and the first word is lower case and the rest upper case (it also switches off *Caps Lock*).

Task 4: Correcting spelling

For this task, in checking spelling, open the document **Centre**.

1   Click on the ▏**Spelling and Grammar**▕ button and check your spelling.

2   If you correct any errors save the document before closing it.

3   Try this with other files you have created, e.g. **Usage**, **Termref** and **Qdesign**.

Task 5: Making an AutoCorrect entry

1   Choose **Tools-AutoCorrect** and select the **AutoCorrect** tab. See that the **Replace text as you type** check box is checked. You will see that Word already has quite a comprehensive list of spelling and keying mistakes and their corrections.

2   In the **Replace:** box type 'usualy' (this is an example of a common mistake).

3   In the **With:** box type 'usually' (the correct spelling) and click on ▏**Add**▕. Click on ▏**OK**▕.

4   In a new document that you do not save experiment with misspelling this word. You may add other words that you commonly mistype, which are not already in the ▏**AutoCorrect**▕ list. Try adding 'item' to replace 'utem'.

Note that if you click on the AutoCorrect button in the **Spelling and grammar** dialog box Word will add your mistake and the selected change to the list.

Using the Thesaurus

The Thesaurus can be used to add variety and interest to your work. A thesaurus finds synonyms and related words. The Thesaurus is used for one word at a time. Place the insertion point in the appropriate word and then choose **Tools-Language-Thesaurus** (shortcut key *Shift/F7*). The **Thesaurus** dialog box appears.

The word that was selected appears in the **Looked Up:** box. Underneath this is the **Meanings:** box, which lists related words and indicates whether these words are nouns or verbs. Next to the **Looked Up:** box is a **Replace with Synonym:** box, which contains a list of synonyms for the selected word. You can replace the selected word with any of the words listed by clicking on the word. It will then appear in the text box at the top of the list and clicking on the **Replace** button will put it into the document in place of the word selected.

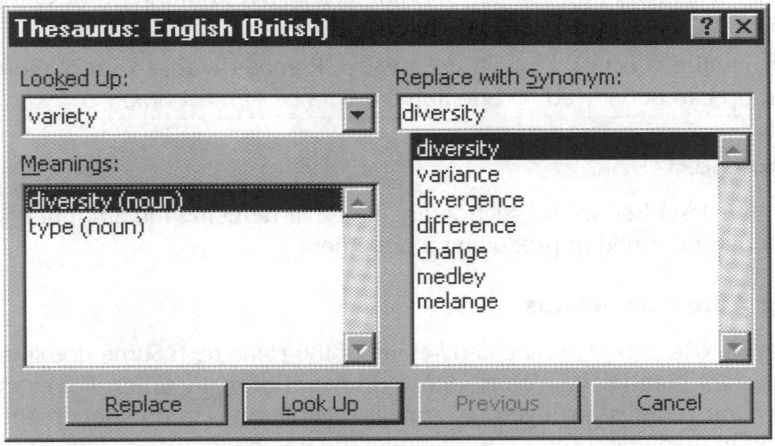

If the list of synonyms is not extensive enough then the Thesaurus can be used to find synonyms for the word in the **Looked Up:** box. To do this, click on the **Look Up** button. This may be repeated until a suitable synonym is found.

The thesaurus keeps a list of all the words you have looked up. To return to a previous word open the **Looked Up:** list box, by clicking on the arrow at the end of the box. Words that you have previously looked up are displayed and the required word can be chosen from the list.

Task 6: Using the Thesaurus

Key the following text into a new document and save it as **Promote**.

> Chelmer Leisure and Recreation Centre has a small promotional budget with which the management can use as they see fit. In the event of a new fitness suite being opened at the centre a great deal of effort must be channelled into creating awareness of the new facility to the potential customer.
>
> The centre is a local authority facility which opens up a range of areas for promotional activities. Other local amenities provide excellent space to promote the new facility. Libraries, other sports facilities, Town Halls and Theatres are venues where any promotional material advertising the new facility can be placed.
>
> Local papers are an excellent promotional tool in the area. There are two popular local papers which are issued weekly and circulated throughout the area. These are the Herald, which is sold throughout the Borough and the Advertiser which is a free newspaper.

Using the Thesaurus investigate synonyms for the following words: deal, creating, range, popular.

1 Place the insertion point in the word to be investigated.

2 Use **Tools-Language-Thesaurus**.

3 Consider whether a replacement should be selected from the list of synonyms.

4 Investigate the effect of 'looking up' a word. Remember that a list of words looked up can be viewed by opening the **Looked Up:** list box.

Using AutoText

The activities described in this section are aimed at reducing the amount of keying that might be performed in producing a document.

Creating AutoText entries

Word uses AutoText to save repeated keying of the same text. Some documents contain text (and/or graphics) which is repeated several or many times. For example, a company name, address or logo may appear several times in one document or may be required in many documents. By defining the name, address or logo as an AutoText entry it may be recalled at any point in any document with a simple keying action. To take a simple example, the text '*Yours sincerely*' appears at the end of many business letters. If many letters are to be typed then defining this as an AutoText entry would help to save time keying.

Word maintains a list of AutoText entries, which you can add to or delete from. An AutoText entry may be text, graphics or a mixture of text and graphics. You can save text or graphics that you use often as an AutoText entry, then you can easily insert the text or graphics into a document with a simple keying action, rather than retyping or using copy and paste.

Making an AutoText entry

First type in the text that you intend to make into an AutoText entry. Check the spelling is correct and select the text. Choose **Insert-AutoText-AutoText** and the **AutoCorrect** dialog box appears.

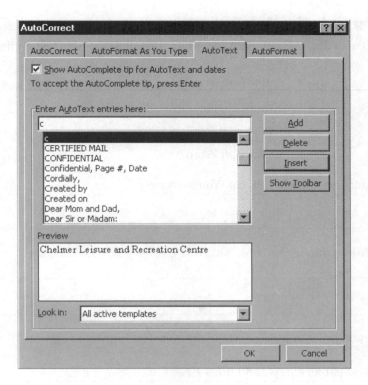

In the **Enter AutoText entries here:** box type a name for the AutoText entry, in this example c for Chelmer Leisure and Recreation Centre. Then click on the **Add** button.

Using an AutoText entry

The simplest method of using an AutoText entry is to type the AutoText name followed immediately by *F3*, i.e. typing c and pressing *F3* would produce the text Chelmer Leisure and Recreation Centre.

Alternatively, if you forget your AutoText names (for example, ys could be the glossary name for Yours sincerely) then use **Insert-AutoText**. In the dialog box will be a list of your previously defined AutoText entries. Type or select the AutoText name you wish to use and click on the **Insert** button.

AutoText prompts

You may have noticed that as you begin to type some words, for example, days of the week, Word prompts you with the completed word or phase. This is another way in which AutoText works. If instead of using c as the AutoText name for Chelmer Leisure and Recreation Centre the full text was used as the name then as you began to type Chelmer you would be prompted with the full text. You may have both names defined so that you can either use *c/F3* or expect to be prompted each time you type Chelmer.

Task 7: Creating and using AutoText entries

Open a new document and try setting up and using the following AutoText entries.

AutoText name	AutoText entry
ys	Yours sincerely
yf	Yours faithfully
ms	Microsoft Word

1   Type out the AutoText entry in full, e.g. Yours sincerely.

2   Select this text.

3   Use **Insert-AutoText** and in the **Enter AutoText entries here:** box type the AutoText name, e.g. ys.

4   Click on   **Add** .

5   Move the insertion point to a place where the AutoText entry is to appear.

6   Type the AutoText name, e.g. ys, and press *F3*

7   Type out the AutoText entry in full, e.g. Yours faithfully.

8   Select this text. Use **Insert-AutoText**; accept Yours faithfully as the name for the AutoText entry and click on   **Add** .

9   Start typing Yours faithfully and you should be prompted when you reach the f of faithfully, press *Enter* to accept the prompt.

Experiment with creating other AutoText entries. Do not save this document.

Task 8: Editing an AutoText entry

Add the following paragraph to the document **Promote** created earlier in this unit.

1   After typing new fitness suite select it

2   Use **Insert-AutoText** to define it as an AutoText entry with the name **n**.

3   Next time this needs to be keyed in simply type n followed by F3.

This form of advertising, i.e. posters, advertisements in local papers, offers a direct link with the public. The money that is spent now to promote the new fitness suite is done so in the hope of increasing usage. The outcome of this form of promotion is uncertain but the main aims are to

- create awareness of the new fitness suite
- inform the public of the services on offer at the centre
- educate/inform of the benefits of the new fitness suite.

Working with windows

What you will learn in this unit

When using a word processor such as Word it is likely that on some occasions you will be creating more than one document at one time. This module explains how to manage and work with more than one open document. At the end of this module you should be familiar with

■ using Windows

■ moving text between documents

■ setting up and using a document template.

Working in a Windows environment makes it possible for different portions of a document to be viewed on the screen at the same time. It also makes it possible to work with more than one document at once.

What you need

To complete this unit you will need

■ the document file **Termref** created in Unit 3.

■ the document file **Centre** created in Unit 5.

■ the document file **Usage** created in Unit 5.

Splitting the document window

By splitting the document window different parts of the same document can be seen on the screen at the same time. This is useful if the portion being written refers to an earlier portion. Viewing the earlier portion while writing the current portion can save scrolling up and down through the document. An earlier part of the document may be copied to a later part and this task is simplified by viewing both parts of the document on screen at the same time.

To split the document

■ move the mouse pointer to the small bar at the top of the vertical scrollbar. The pointer changes shape to two horizontal lines with arrows

■ while the pointer is this shape click and drag a horizontal line downwards. Position the line approximately halfway down the document window and release.

At the right-hand edge of the window the vertical scrollbar now appears as two separate scrollbars, one for each portion of the split. It is possible to scroll each split portion independently thereby positioning an earlier portion of the document on the screen at the same time as a later one. Note that each portion has its own ruler.

To remove a split

■ move the mouse pointer to the bar between the two vertical scrollbars. The pointer changes shape to two horizontal lines with arrows

■ while the pointer is this shape click and drag the split line upwards. Position the line at the top of the document screen area and release.

More than one window onto the same document

Another way of viewing two parts of a document at the same time is to use more than one window. This can provide more flexibility and be useful when working with larger documents. If, for example, you wished to refer to more than one page of the document then it would be useful to be able to switch between several 'views' of the different pages.

To set up another window onto the document use **Window-New Window**. Word redisplays the document and the title of the document is altered by the addition of :2. This is the window number. Every time **Window-New Window** is used a new window onto the document is created.

To see a list of the windows that have been created open the **Window** menu. The list of open windows is in the lower section of this menu. To switch to another window simply click on the name of the appropriate one in the **Window** list.

File-Close closes the document and all associated windows. To close a document's specific windows use the control menu symbol associated with that window. If the document fills the application window it is leftmost in the menu bar; if the document window is smaller than the application window then it is at the leftmost of the document title bar. The shortcut key to close a document window is *Ctrl/w*.

To view several windows on the screen at the same time use **Window-Arrange All**. The windows can be positioned by moving and sizing them. However, the screen can become rather cluttered. For this reason it is advisable to have no more than four windows open. Only one window can be active at once. If the default Windows colours are being used then the active window has a blue title bar. To change the active window simply click on the one to be made active.

A document window may be in one of three 'Windows' states, i.e. it may be maximised (fills application window), 'restored' (smaller than the application window) or minimised (shown as a small button at the bottom of the application's workspace). You can control the 'Window' state of your document window by clicking on the
minimize , **restore** and **maximize** buttons.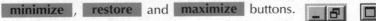

Cutting and copying between windows

Copy or cut and paste operations can be carried out between windows. First switch to or make active the window containing the portion of the document that is to be cut or copied. Select the section and use **Edit-Cut** (*Ctrl/x*) or **Edit-Copy** (*Ctrl/c*) to transfer it to the clipboard.

Next switch to the window into which the contents of the clipboard are to be pasted by using the **Window** menu, or make it active by clicking in it. Position the insertion point and choose **Edit-Paste** (or *Ctrl/v*).

Working with more than one document

All that has been described about using more than one window into a document can be applied to using more than one document. Instead of using **Window-New Window** to open more windows onto the document, use **File-Open** to open all the documents required. To see a list of all open documents open the **Window** menu, and use **Window-Arrange All** if you wish to see all document windows arranged on the screen at the same time.

Copy or cut and paste operations can be carried out as described previously. Note that portions that are pasted into a document retain the font and formatting that was applied in the original document.

Task 1: Working with windows

To perform this task close any documents that you may have open using **File-Close**. When all documents are closed the application workspace is empty of documents or minimised document buttons.

1 Open the file **Termref**.

2 Open the file **Centre**.

3 Choose **Window-Arrange All**. Both documents should be visible on the screen, each occupying its own window taking up half the screen display.

4 Open the file **Usage**. Open the **Window** menu and notice that all of the open documents are listed. Select **Arrange All**.

5 The screen has become cluttered so close **Termref** (click anywhere in the **Termref** document window to make it active). Click on the control menu box for that window and chose **Close**.

6 Use **Window-Arrange All** to reposition the remaining document windows.

7 To copy text from one window to another, make **Centre** active by clicking in its window. Press *Ctrl/End* to move the insertion point to the end of the document.

8 Make **Usage** active. Highlight the first paragraph and use **Edit-Copy**.

9 Make **Centre** active, check that the insertion point is at the end of the document, and use **Edit-Paste**.

10 Close the documents but do not save the changes.

11 Open two of the documents again and experiment with minimising, maximising and restoring them. If you can't find a document because it is hidden behind another document window then open the **Window** menu to locate it.

12 Close these two documents.

Creating templates

A template is a predefined format for a document. Many business documents such as letters, memos, forms and reports have set formats. A template can be used to define not only standard text but also aspects such as the font, borders, page size and orientation. Once a template has been created it can be recalled and used to produce the required document. This saves time and ensures consistency.

Word comes with many predefined templates and several Wizards to help you create documents such as letters and memos. To create most documents the 'normal document' template Normal.dot is used. This is the template that you have been using to create your documents. If a document is started using **File-New** then a dialog box containing the names of the templates appears. These are grouped by type, which you select by clicking on the appropriate tab. Under the **General** tab you can select the normal template file by choosing **Blank Document**. Template files have the extension .dot and are stored in the word template folder.

Word provides other template files, such as a standard letter and memo, and it is possible to customise these. However, Task 2 will concentrate on producing a custom template based on the normal template. The template will contain standard text. Standard text is often referred to as boilerplate text.

Task 2: Creating a template

There are several ways of creating a template; the one that will be used for this task will create a template from the document that is being worked on. The template will be set up based upon Word's Normal template, which is the one usually used for document creation.

1 Start a new document and key in the text on the following page, leaving the prices blank.

2 Save this as a template rather than a document. Use **File-Save**, and in the **Save As** dialog box open the **Save as Type:** box choose Document Template. Add Prices to the end of the suggested filename in the **File name** box and click on **Save**. Close the template document.

3 To use this template for the creation of a new document (e.g. when the prices change), start a new document using **File-New**.

4 Select from the **General** tab in the dialog box and click on the icon labelled Chelmer Leisure and Recreation Centre Prices.

6 The (boilerplate) text and formatting will appear and the prices can be filled in and the document saved and printed in the usual manner.

Chelmer Leisure and Recreation Centre
MultiGym

Price per session

Adult

Junior

Concessionary

Club Adult

Club Junior

Template files can be recalled and edited, by using **File-Open** and selecting **Document Template** in the **Files of type:** list box. Template files are normally stored in the MSOffice Template (or Winword Template) folder, not in your working folder. If you use a networked version of Word then custom templates may be stored in an alternative folder. Check with your network manager.

Tab stops

What you will learn in this unit

This unit focuses on activities associated with the creation of tables of text and numbers using tab stops. At the end of this unit you will be able to

- use and change default tab stops to set up a simple table

- set custom tab stops

- use different types of tab stops

- insert tab stops in an existing document.

 Familiarity with such operations will allow you to construct documents where it is frequently necessary to present text or numbers in columns, such as tables of numbers or text, curriculum vitae, questionnaires and forms. Unit 9 explores a further way of setting up such tables using a feature called Tables.

Important note

It is frequently necessary to be able to present text or numbers as lists in columns. If you are accustomed to using a typewriter you may have used the _Spacebar_ to align text. **Do not use the** _Spacebar_ to format or align text with a word processor. The _Spacebar_ should only be used to insert a space between words. If you attempt to use the _Spacebar_ to align text in columns, this will impede later formatting and although columns may appear aligned on the screen they will not be aligned when printed out. Modern printers use proportionally spaced fonts where different letters are allocated different amounts of space. It is essential to use the facilities described in this and Units 9 to 11 in order to produce effective tables.

Default tab stops

The simplest way to create text that is lined up in columns is to use tab stops. If you inspect the Ruler, (if the Ruler is not displayed then display it by selecting **View-Ruler**), you will see that Word provides default left tab stops at approximately every half inch. Text can be aligned at these tab stops simply by pressing the _Tab_ key to move to the next tab stop position.

The default tab stops can be changed by choosing **Format-Tabs**, and making appropriate changes in the **Default Tab Stops** box in the **Tabs** dialog box, and then choosing OK .

Task 1: Using default tab stops

With a new document open

1 Type in the following text, using Courier New 12pt, working one line at a time and using the *tab* key to move between one column and the next.

2 Press the *Enter* key to move on to a new line.

3 Finally format the headings as shown in the sample.

Opening Times

Health Suite

```
Monday      9.00am - 9.00pm   Ladies Only
Tuesday     9.00am - 9.00pm   Mixed
Wednesday 9.30am - 9.00pm     Mixed
Thursday    9.00am - 1.00pm   Ladies Only
            1.00pm - 9.00pm   Mixed
Friday      9.00am - 9.00pm   Men Only
Saturday    9.00am - 1.00pm   Men Only
            1.00pm - 5.00pm   Mixed
Sunday      9.00am - 5.00pm   Mixed
```

Now change the default tab stops so that the final column is further away from the times, by choosing **Format-Tabs** and iusing the **Default Tab Stops** box and increasing the distance between the default tab stops to 1.5cm, and notice the effect on your document. Note that if you set the distance between default tab stops to 2cm the document loses its columnar apperance. This is because some words e.g. Wednesday are longer than others e.g. Friday and the longer words obscure a tab stop whereas the shorter ones don't. To avoid this it is better to set custom tab stops on the ruler as will be seen in the next section. Save this document as **Times**.

Types of tab stops

There are four types of tab stops: left, centre, right and decimal. Each of these may be set by clicking on the **Tab** button at the left-hand side of the ruler, which in the default mode is shown as a left tab. Clicking on this button, causes it to cycle through the different tab types.

Tab button	Tab type	Tab function
L	**Left**	Text is aligned with its left edge on the tab stops; this is the usual typewriter type of tab and is the default. This is useful for aligning columns of words.

Tab button	Tab type	Tab function
[icon]	**Centre**	Text is centred beneath the tab stop. This can be useful in advertisements and other documents where you wish to display text.
[icon]	**Right**	Text is aligned with its right edge under the tab stop. This is useful for numbers that do not contain a decimal point and for text that must be aligned in a column, against, say, the right margin.
[icon]	**Decimal**	Numbers are aligned with the decimal point beneath the tab stop. Clearly useful for numbers, particularly money.

Setting tab stops with the ruler and the mouse

It is easiest in the first instance if you insert tab stops before creating text, rather than try to add them later, although this is perfectly possible once you are confident with the use of tab stops.

To add a tab stop

- select the paragraphs to which you want to add tab stops, or position the insertion point where you want the formatting with tab stops to start, as you type the document

- click on one of the `Tab` button until it displays the tab type that you wish to use, i.e. left, right, centre or decimal

- point to where you wish to place the tab on the ruler and click to place a tab stop at that point. The tab should appear on the ruler as a tiny version of the tab symbol on the button.

This procedure can be repeated to add other tab stops.

Ruler without custom tab stops; the default tabs can just be seen on the lower part of the ruler at half inch intervals.

Ruler showing custom tabs. There is a left tab at 1.5cm, a centre tab at 4.5cm, a right tab at 7.5cm and a decimal tab at 11.5cm.

Clearing custom tab stops with the ruler

To clear custom tab stops

- select the paragraph that contains the tab stops to be cleared

■ on the ruler drag the marker for the tab stop that you want to remove down out of the ruler.

Customising tab stops with the tabs command

The Tabs command offers a further way of controlling various aspects of tab stops. With the appropriate paragraph selected, choose **Format-Tabs**. This displays the Tabs dialog box.

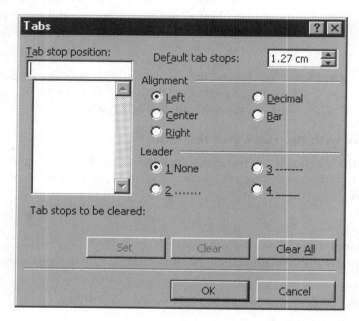

This box allows you to change the format of existing tabs or to add any new tabs. Formatting will be applied to the tab displayed in the box at the top of the Tabs stop position: box. You can enter a new tab position in this box, or display an existing tab by selecting it from further down the Tabs stop position: box. For each tab it is possible to set its alignment and leader. A leader is a series of characters that appear before the text at the tab stop, such as a series of dots. After specifying these characteristics, click on the **Set** button. The position of the default stops may be adjusted and, stops may be cleared using the **Clear** or **Clear All** buttons. Exit with **OK** to accept new settings.

Task 2: Setting tab stops

1   With the document called **Times** open that you used in Task 1, move the pointer to the end of the existing text and reset the tabs to cater for the following text.

2   You should set the following tabs

   ■ a left tab at 2.5cm (1.00")

   ■ a centre tab at 6.5cm (2.50")

■ a right tab at 10.25cm (4.00")

Health Suite Passcards

Gold Passcard. Use of all our facilities including the
Health Suite, Fitness Suite, Pool and Oasis.

3 Month	Gold Pass	£85.00
6 Month	Gold Pass	£150.00
12 Month	Gold Pass	£275.00

---

3   Click on the **Tab** button on the ruler and choose the appropriate tab type.

4   Point to where you wish to place the tab on the ruler and click to place a tab stop at that point.

5   Type in the text, using the *Tab* key to move between tab stops.

Now re-format the tabs.

6   Select the text that you have just entered and use the **Format-Tabs** command, to display the **Tabs** dialog box on screen.

7   Select the first tab, change its alignment to **Right** and introduce a leader with
....

8   Choose **Set** , then **OK** .

9   Note the effect that this has on your document.

10 Save the document.

Task 3: Inserting tabs in an existing document

This task asks you to insert a new paragraph with new tabs in the middle of a document. Newcomers to word processing often have difficulty with this, so it is worth practising.

With the document called **Times** open

1   Move the insertion point to a position between the two pieces of text that you entered for Task 1 and 2.

2   Open up some space by pressing *Enter*.

3   Move the insertion point back to the top of this space.

4   Prepare to insert the following table.

Fitness Suite		
Monday	8.00am - 8.00pm	
	8.00pm - 9.00pm	Super Circuit
Tuesday	9.00am - 9.00pm	
Wednesday	9.30am - 8.00pm	
	8.00am - 9.00pm	Super Circuit
Thursday	9.00am - 9.00pm	
Friday	9.00am - 9.00pm	
Saturday	9.00am - 5.00pm	
Sunday	9.00am - 5.00pm	

5   Set a centre tab at 5cm (2") and a left tab at 9cm (3.1") using the ruler.

6   Enter text using the *Tab* key to move between stops.

7   Now move up and down the document and examine the different tab stops as they are applied to different parts of the document.

8   Save the document and close it.

Creating a table

What you will learn in this unit

This unit explains how to use the Tables feature to create tables of text. The Tables feature is a more sophisticated way of creating the tables that you created in Unit 8 with tab stops. Tables created with the Tables feature are easy to format. Unit 10 goes on to demonstrate how Tables can be used with borders and shading to create forms. At the end of this unit you will be able to

■ set up a simple table

■ enter text in a table

■ select text in a table and perform simple formatting operations

■ sort text in a table.

Tables are an easy way to arrange and adjust columns of text and numbers, and are much more flexible than tabs. Once you have taken a few moments to master tables you will wonder how you ever managed without them. A table can be inserted at any point in your text. A table offers an easy way to group paragraphs side by side and to arrange text beside related graphics on a page. Tables can be used to organise information in the data documents that are merged to create form letters, mailing labels and other merged documents. By adding borders and shading to a table you can create many types of forms. Tables allow easy transfer of data between Excel and Word. If you create a table in Word, you can insert the table in an Excel worksheet and work with it as you would with any other spreadsheet data; the converse is also possible. Insert an Excel worksheet into a Word document and you can work with the data just as you would with a Word table. However, more of these ambitious applications of tables later.

Setting up a simple table

To set up a table

1   position the insertion point where you want to insert the table

2   click on the **Insert Table** button on the toolbar ▦

3   on the **Insert Table** button grid, drag the pointer to select the number of columns and rows that you want the new table to have

4   release the mouse button to insert the table

or

1   choose **Table-Insert Table**

2 in the **Number of Columns:** box, type or select a number indicating how many columns you want

3 choose OK .

or

1 choose **Table-Draw Table**. Drag the drawing tool to create the outside box of the table. Release the mouse button

2 drag the drawing tool to draw in vertical and horizontal lines to complete the grid for this table

Note: You can add rows and adjust column widths later to suit your needs. It is usually a good idea to accept the defaults on your first try.

Entering text in a table

Once you have created a table, you should have an empty table, with the insertion point in the first cell so that you can start typing. Mostly you can move the insertion point and select and edit text in the same way as in the rest of your document. As you enter text the boxes will expand to accommodate it.

To	Operation
Start new paragraphs in a cell	Press *Enter*
Move to the next cell	Press *Tab*
Move to the first cell in the next row	Press *Tab* in the rightmost cell
Add another row of cells	Press *Tab* in the last cell in the table
Leave the table	Place the insertion point after the table before typing
Insert a **tab** stop	With the pointer in the box in which you wish to insert a tab stop, click on the Tab button to select the type of tab stop, then, while depressing *Ctrl*, click on the ruler where you wish to insert the tab stop
Change the column width	Drag the cell border of the column whose width you want to change

Note: When you create a table, Word displays gridlines between cells. These help you to see which cell you are working in. These can be hidden, by, for instance, choosing **Table-Hide Gridlines**. It is usually best to work with the *gridlines* on. Gridlines will not be printed.

Task 1: Creating a table

1 Open a new document.

2   Type in the heading below.

3   Create a table either by using the **Table-Insert Table** command or the **Table** button, with three columns and one row.

4   Enter the text into the columns, moving between columns using the *Tab* key. Also use the *Tab* key to create each new row in the table. If you need to adjust the width of the columns do so by dragging the column boundary. Do not try to format the column headings yet.

5   The table as displayed has borders. Remove these by selecting **Format-Borders and Shading**, and then clicking on None, followed by **OK** . This leaves grey gridlines, which will not be printed.

6   Save the document as **Fatlim** and close it.

How much fat is the limit?		
Type of fat	Saturated	Other fats
12.5st(80kg) man		
Inactive	28g	68g
Quite active	35g	82g
Very active	42g	97g
9.5st(61kg) woman		
Inactive	22g	51g
Quite active	27g	63g
Very active	31g	74g

Selecting within a table

In order to edit, format or add a border to certain parts of a table it is necessary to select specific parts of the table. Remember that the selected area will be highlighted in black. Selection can be achieved as indicated below.

To select	Operation
Cell	Click in the cell's selection area, which is a strip down its left side where the mouse pointer changes to a right pointing arrow
Any rectangular area of cells	Place the mouse pointer anywhere in the top left cell and drag down and to the right until the area you want is selected

To select	Operation
Row	Click in the row selection bar to the left of the row, or double click in any cell's selection area in the row. Alternatively, choose **Table-Select Row**
Column	Click in the column selection bar at the top of the column, or click anywhere in the column with the right mouse button. Alternatively, choose **Table-Select Column**
Whole table	Point to the leftmost column, hold down the right mouse button, and drag across the table. Alternatively, choose **Table-Select Table**

Once you have selected text within a table it is possible to apply formatting, moving, copying and other operations to text in the same way as with text elsewhere in the document. For example, with appropriate cells selected, the following operations may be performed.

To	Do this
Delete	Choose **Edit-Cut**
Copy	Choose **Edit-Copy** or **Edit-Cut**. Move the insertion point and choose **Edit-Paste**
Display the headings in each column in bold	Select the first row of the table, containing the headings and click on the **Bold** button
Align text within a cell	Set tab stops
Adjust the alignment of paragraphs within cells	Click the **alignment formatting** buttons
Move a row of cells	Select the row. Drag the selected rows to the new location. Position the mouse pointer at the beginning of the selected rows, then release the left mouse button
Sort a table on the basis of the contents in a given column	Select the sort column. Choose **Table-Sort**. The **Sort** dialog box will be displayed. Select the appropriate column and then for type choose **Text**. Select an ascending or a descending sort. Click on **OK**. Rows are ordered alphabetically according to the text in the sorted column

Task 2: Formatting a table

Open the document **Fatlim**. Format the column headings by first selecting them and then applying appropriate formatting as above.

1   To select the first cell, click on its left side.

2   Click on the **Bold** and **Italic** buttons to format the text.

3   Repeat this operation with the other cells whose text requires formatting.

When finished **Fatlim** should appear as it does in this unit. Save the file.

Task 3: Sorting a table and adding rows

In a new document:

1   Insert a table with three columns and one row using **Table-Insert Table**.

2   Adjust the column widths by dragging them to accommodate the addresses shown below.

3   Insert the addresses into the cells.

4   Sort the table on the basis of the name column contents, by selecting that column, and choosing **Table-Sort** and appropriate options from the **Sort** dialog box. Click on **OK**. Rows should be ordered alphabetically according to the text in the sorted column.

5   To add a row for column headings place the pointer in the top left-hand corner and use **Table-Insert Rows**.

6   Enter the text of the column headings.

7   Save the document as **Address**.

Supplier	Address	Telephone
Universal Gym (Europe) Ltd	Hutton, Brentwood, Essex, CM13 1XA	0277-221122
Atlanta Sports Industries Ltd	Atlanta House, Rotherway, Euroway Estate, Maltby, Rotherham, S66 8QN	0709-700555
Physique Training Equipment Ltd	Bankfield Mill, Greenfield Road, Colne, Lancashire, BB8 9PD.	0282-863300

Creating forms using tables

What you will learn in this unit

This unit continues the theme of Unit 9, the use of tables. It introduces some more sophisticated editing features and demonstrates how tables can be used to create forms and other more complex documents. At the end of this unit you will be able to

- format a table, by for instance, inserting and deleting rows
- use table formatting to create a simple form
- put existing text into a table, so that it can be manipulated as a table.

What you need

To complete this unit you will need

- the document file **Times** created in Unit 8.

Editing a table

As you develop a table you will find that you may need to insert or delete a row or column, delete or insert single cells, or split a table into two separate tables. This may be achieved as shown in the following table.

To	Do this
Insert a row	Select the row below where you want to insert a new row, and click the **Insert Rows** button on the tool-bar, or choose **Table-Insert Rows**. To insert a new row at the bottom of the table place the cursor below the last row of the table and choose **Table-Insert Rows**, or alternatively place the cursor in the right-most cell of the last row and press *Tab*
Insert a column	Select the column to the right of where you wish to add the new column and click the table icon on the toolbar or choose **Table-Insert Columns**. To enter a column to the right of the table, place the cursor to the right of the table and choose **Table-Select Column** then **Table-Insert Columns**
Delete a row	Select the row or rows and choose **Table-Delete Rows**
Delete a column	Select the column or columns and choose **Table-Delete Columns**

Insert a single cell	Select a cell and choose **Table-Insert Cells**. Decide where to shift the displaced cells i.e. to either to the right on the row or down the column. Choose either **Insert Entire Row** or **Insert Entire Column**, if you are accidentally using the wrong command
Delete a single cell	Proceed as for inserting a single cell, choosing whether to close up the row or column
Split a table into two separate tables	Select the row which is to become the top row of the second table and choose **Table-Split Table**. A normal paragraph will be inserted to break the table into two parts. This command offers a way of inserting normal text above a table at the start of a document
Split a cell into two cells	Select the cell, and choose **Table-Split Cells** In the **Split Cells** dialog box choose the number of columns (or rows). Click on **OK** . Cells can be merged in a similar way using **Table-Merge Cells**

Task 1: Editing a table

This task asks you to use some of the formatting skills that you have learnt in using tables to design a form. There are a number of tips for form design.

■ Remember the form's purpose, and keep the gaps the right size.

■ Leave bigger gaps for manual filling.

■ Request all necessary information but no unnecessary information.

■ Ask for information in a logical sequence.

■ The headings should be clear and designed to help the reader to understand the form.

Taking all of these points into consideration, we wish to design a form for application of membership for a Health and Fitness Club, which looks something like the one shown below, but which may be formatted slightly differently if you choose. I have used borders to print the gridlines so that you can see where they are positioned. You do not need to do this.

1   Type in the first three rows.

2   Justify and format these three rows as you choose.

3   Insert a table with four columns using **Table-Insert Table**.

4   Start to enter the labels. You may need to drag the column boundaries to a position so that the labels are displayed sensibly.

5   To enter 'For Office Use Only' you will need to widen the first column on this row only.

6   Select the appropriate cell.

7   Drag the column boundary to accommodate the text.

8   When you have completed this first part of the table, move the cursor below the table, press *Enter* to insert a row, and insert a further table with **Table-Insert Table**, immediately below the first table. This table should have six columns of approximately equal width. You may need to drag the column widths to align the two tables. In addition you should delete any space between the two tables.

9   Enter the final text into this table.

10 Format all of the labels by displaying them in bold.

11 Save as **Appform**. We will return to this document later to improve it.

Chelmer Leisure and Recreation Centre
Health and Fitness Club
Membership Application Form

Name				
Address				
		Telephone		
Occupation		Date of Birth		
Sporting		Date of Joining		
Interests				
For Office Use Only				
Date Subs Due		Subs Paid		Mem.Cat

Table formatting

The table formatting command **Table-Cell Height and Width** allows you to format your table. The Column tab allows you to specify width of columns and space between columns, for each column in turn.

The **Row** tab covers many aspects of table formatting, including

- indent from left: moves the whole table or selection to the right to leave an indent space at the left

- height of rows m-n: normally set to **Auto**, which gives a row height sufficient for the highest cell. This can also be specified

- alignment   can be set to left, centre or right to align selected rows or the whole table.

These commands, together with other formatting that is available for all text, offer a wide range of formatting options. To view the effect of formatting on the table, do not forget to view your document in Page Layout view.

Task 2: Formatting a table

1   View **Appform** in Page Layout view.

2   Select the table.

3   Using **Table-Cell Height and Width** and the Column tab, change the space between columns to 0.5 cm.

4   Select the whole table and, using **Table-Cell Height and Width** and the Row tab, select centre alignment to centre the table on the page. Save the document as **Appform**.

Putting existing text into a table

If you already have a table laid out using tab characters, or some columns of text separated by commas, this can be converted into a table by

■ selecting the original table

■ choosing **Table-Convert Text to Table**.

Word will examine the existing text and convert it into a table with suitable column widths. If Word can not determine how to convert the text, it displays a dialog box listing different conversion options.

If the resultant table is not as you would like it, remember to use **Edit-Undo** before taking any other action.

Alternatively, a table may be converted into regular text paragraphs. Simply select the rows of the table to be converted to text, and choose **Table-Convert Table to Text**. Select an appropriate Separate text with option and choose **OK**.

Task 3: Turning text into tables

1   Open the document **Times**. This has existing tab stops.

2   Select the section showing opening times.

3   Choose **Table-Convert Text toTable**. The text should appear as a table with the gridlines displayed.

4   You may need to drag the column boundaries so that the text is all displayed in the most effective way.

5   Save the document as **Times1**.

Task 4: Designing a simple questionnaire

We now want to start to design a simple questionnaire and to be a little more ambitious in our use of tables. The questionnaire that we wish to start to design is shown below: I have printed borders so that you can see where the gridlines are, but you do not need to do this yet.

Chelmer Leisure and Recreation Centre
Market Research Questionnaire

Occupation		Sex (M/F)		
Age Band		**Smoking**		
Under 20		Non-smoker		
21-30		Pipe and/or cigar		
31-40		Under 10 cigs a day		
41-50		20 cigs a day		
51-60		30 cigs a day		
Over 60				

Which of the following would you be interested in attending? (Please Tick)	*Not at all*	*Somewhat*	*Very much*
Workshops on:			
Diet/Nutrition			
Stress Management			
Exercise			
Health Screening:			
Coronary Risk Assessment			
Cholesterol Check			
Blood Pressure Check			
Flexibility			
Strength			
Dietary Analysis			
Aerobic Fitness			

Please return this questionnaire to Chelmer Leisure and Recreation Centre. Thank you for your co-operation.

1   Open a new document.

2   Type in the title, format and centre it.

3 Place the insertion point on a new line and choose **Table-Insert Table**, and create a table with four columns.

4 Enter the text in the table down to 'Over 60', using the *Tab* key to move between cells.

5 Press the *Tab* key a few times to create a few empty cells. Leave one blank row.

6 Select these empty cells and drag the column boundaries on the bottom part of the table so that the cells will accommodate the text.

7 Enter the text in the lower part of the table into the new cells.

8 Format the text as appropriate

9 Save the document as **Question**.

Applying borders and shading to text

What you will learn in this unit

This unit introduces the use of borders and shading. The first few tasks help you to learn how to apply borders and shading to plain text. Later in the unit we attempt some much more sophisticated use of borders and shading when we seek to apply them to text in tables. Borders and shading are very useful for enhancing the appearance of a document, or for highlighting specific parts of the document. At the end of this unit you will be able to

- use Table AutoFormat to apply quick borders and shading
- apply and format borders to text
- remove and change borders
- apply borders to text in tables
- apply shading to text
- apply shading to text in tables.

What you need

To complete this unit you will need

- the document file **Address** created in Unit 9
- the document file **Openday** created in Unit 4
- the document file **Appform** created in Unit 10
- the document file **Question** created in Unit 10.

Applying borders and shading to text

You will have observed that both the form and the questionnaire designed in Unit 10 require additional formatting. This can be achieved by the use of borders and shading.

The design of a document can be improved significantly if borders, lines and shading are used sparingly. Borders and shading can be applied to paragraphs of text, graphics or the cells in a table. With a colour printer, you can print coloured borders and shading. This unit introduces the basics of borders and shading and leaves you to experiment further with the immense potential of these features.

Quick borders and shading: Table AutoFormat

A quick way to apply borders and shading to a table is to use Table-Table AutoFormat, which displays the Table AutoFormat dialog box. This dialog box lists a series of preset formats, and shows their format through a Preview box. These preset formats can be modified by changing: borders, shading, font, colour and AutoFit. It is also possible to apply special formats to heading rows, first column, last row and last column.

Task 1: Using Table AutoFormat

1 Open the document **Address**.

2 Select the table.

3 Choose Table AutoFormat.

4 Experiment with the different standard formats, until the table resembles the table below.

Supplier	Address	Telephone
Universal Gym (Europe) Ltd	Hutton, Brentwood, Essex, CM13 1XA	0277-221122
Atlanta Sports Industries Ltd	Atlanta House, Rotherway, Euroway Estate, Maltby, Rotherham, S66 8QN	0709-700555
Physique Training Equipment Ltd	Bankfield Mill, Greenfield Road, Colne, Lancashire, BB8 9PD.	0282-863300

Applying and formatting borders

To **apply a border**, select the items to which a border is to be applied, then choose Format-Borders and Shading. This displays the Borders and Shading dialog box. If no text is selected, but the insertion point is in normal text, the border is applied to the paragraph that contains the insertion point.

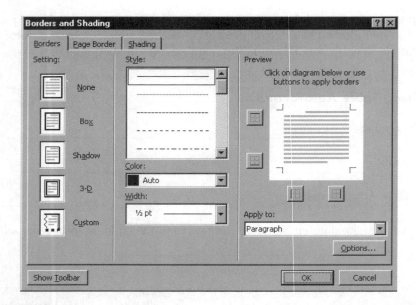

To **apply a box**, click on the box option under **Setting:** and then click a line style under **Style:**. If you want to change the colour of the border, select a colour in the **Color:** box.

To **create a custom border** or to add lines within a box, click the border preview where you want to apply a border or one of the border buttons within the Preview, and then click a line style under **Style:**.

To **change the distance of the border from the text** click on the Options button. Set the distance using the options in the **Border and Shading Options** dialog box.

To change the width of a border, click on the **Width:** box, [icon] and select an appropriate width from the options displayed.

Alternatively, click on the **Border** button on the toolbar to display the Borders list.

Removing and changing borders

To remove or change a border, first select the item that has the border to be removed or changed. Choose **Format-Borders and Shading**. Then

- to remove all borders, click **None** under **Setting**
- to remove one border at a time, click the border you want to remove on the border sample

■ click on OK .

Borders may also be changed by selecting the item with the border to be changed. Choose **Format-Borders and Shading**, and changing the selected options in the **Borders** dialog box.

Task 2: Applying borders

This task encourages you to explore some of the basics of applying borders to text.

1   Open the document **Openday**, that you created in Task 1 of Unit 4.

2   Select all of the text in this document.

3   Choose **Format-Borders and Shading** to display the **Borders and Shading** dialog box.

4   Click on the **Box** option under **Setting:**.

5   Choose a line style e.g. double, under **Style:**.

6   Click on the **Shadow** box. Choose OK

7   Examine, print and save your document as **Openday**.

Task 3: Using borders on forms

This task attempts a more sophisticated use of borders in the use of borders in applications based on tables such as an application form or questionnaire.

1   Open the document **Appform**.

2   Ensure that only the gridlines and text are displayed, and no borders.

3   Create borders around the cells in which data is to be entered, by selecting each cell in turn.

4   Choose **Format-Borders and Shading**.

5   Click on the **Box** option under **Setting:**.

6   Choose a line style under **Style:**. Choose OK .

7   Next select the row with 'For Office Use Only'.

8   Choose **Format-Borders and Shading**.

9 Click on the None option under Setting:.

10 Select the top border by clicking on this border on the sample.

11 Select a double line under Style:.

12 Select the bottom row.

13 Choose Format-Borders and Shading and Grid: under Setting: and an appropriate line. Choose OK .

14 Choose Table-Hide Gridlines and turn off the gridlines so that you can view your formatting and borders.

Chelmer Leisure and Recreation Centre			
Health and Fitness Club			
Membership Application Form			
Name			
Address			
		Telephone	
Occupation		**Date of Birth**	
Sporting		**Date of Joining**	
Interests			

For Office Use Only					
Date Subs Due		**Subs Paid**		**Mem.Cat**	

Applying shading

Shading can be applied to paragraphs or the cells in a table. If you have a colour printer, you can shade tables and paragraphs with colours.

Shading can be used to shade a short section in a newsletter, or an important column of figures in a table. Shading on paragraphs covers the text. Shading in table cells fills the cell.

Remember that shading affects the legibility of the text. In general, light shading of 20% or less is most effective. Small font sizes are difficult to read with shading. The use of bold may improve the text legibility.

Choose Format-Borders and Shading, and clicking on the Shading tab. The Shading dialog box has the following options

- fill: click on one of these boxes to select a black and white shading or a colour for the shading

- patterns-style: click on one of these options to choose the density or style of shading

■ patterns-colour: click on one of these options to select a colour for the pattern in the shading.

Task 4: Applying shading

We wish to improve the questionnaire that we started to design earlier and to add borders and shading. This is a relatively ambitious project and although the basic steps are outlined below you are likely to find that parts of the tables have moved to places where you do not want them. You need to be confident in working with tables to succeed with this task.

Chelmer Leisure and Recreation Centre
Market Research Questionnaire

Occupation		Sex (M/F)	

Age Band		Smoking	
Under 20		Non-smoker	
21-30		Pipe and/or cigar	
31-40		Under 10 cigs a day	
41-50		20 cigs a day	
51-60		30 cigs a day	
Over 60			

Which of the following would you be interested in attending? (Please Tick)	Not at all	Somewhat	Very much
Workshops on:			
Diet/Nutrition			
Stress Management			
Exercise			
Health Screening:			
Coronary Risk Assessment			
Cholesterol Check			
Blood Pressure Check			
Flexibility			
Strength			
Dietary Analysis			
Aerobic Fitness			

Please return this questionnaire to Chelmer Leisure and Recreation Centre. Thank you for your co-operation.

To add borders and shading to the questionnaire:

1 Select the first two lines, i.e. the heading.

2   Choose **Format-Borders and Shading** and then in the **Borders and Shading** dialog box choose an appropriate double line which should be a box by default, and click on **Shadow**.

3   Next select each set of boxes with labels and associated reply boxes and apply a single line border with the Grid.

4   The top two sets of boxes would look better if they were separated. Select the top part of the third column and insert a column using **Table-Insert Cells**, and choosing **Shift cells right**.

5   With the top part of the table selected move the column boundary to make this new column fairly narrow.

6   Select the new column and remove any borders. In so doing you may manage to remove some of the borders that you have just created. Just insert them again. It's all good practice.

7   Now apply shading to each of the cells shown as shaded in the example above. Select the cell, and choose **Format-Borders and Shading** and then click on the Shading tab. This displays the **Shading** dialog box.

8   Choose a **Shading**, say **20%**. Experiment with a style for your shading.

9   Save your document as **Question** and print it.

Special tips for borders and shading

The ways in which you can apply borders and shading are almost endless. Here are just a few ideas that might be useful.

■   Word applies borders to the edges of a selected graphic. If you have **cropped close to the image and need to add space** between the image and the border, select the graphic to display the sizing handles. Press *Shift* and drag the centre handles on each side of the graphic to increase the space between the edge of the graphic and the image.

■   To **place graphics adjacent to one another** place the graphics in a table, and then apply borders to the table cells.

■   To **add a double border to separate column headings from table entries** first apply single borders on all sides of the cell. First select the table, then choose **Format-Borders and Shading** and under **Setting** select **Grid**, then **OK** . Then select the first row of the table and change the line style of the border below the row.

■   You can **apply borders to paragraphs and graphics within a table cell** in addition to the borders that you apply to the cell itself.

■ If you want to **apply the same border to a group of paragraphs**, all paragraphs must have the same indents. Otherwise paragraphs are placed in separate boxes. To place all text in one box, convert the text to a one-column table.

Task 5: Using borders and shading

In this task we wish to create the following table, which summarises a timetable for activities at the leisure centre during the week.

1 Open a new document.

2 Enter the heading, and format and centre the text.

3 Choose Table-Insert Table. Create a table with six columns.

4 Enter the text into the table.

5 Select the table, and apply borders using Format-Borders and Shading. Apply a Grid.

6 Select appropriate cells and apply shading using Format-Borders and Shading.

7 Save the document as **Timetble**.

Chelmer Leisure and Recreation Centre
ACTIVITY PROGRAMME

FITNESS SUITE	Monday	Tuesday	Wednesday	Thursday	Friday
Daytime					
10.00-11.00am	Ladies Aerobics	Mens Multi-gym	Ladies Aerobics		Body Conditioning
11.00-12.00pm	Weight Training			Weight Training	Step Aerobics
2.00-3.00pm		Ladies Multi-gym	Body Conditioning	Step Aerobics	Mens Multi-gym
3.00-4.00pm	Body conditioning		Weight Training	Multi-gym	
Evening					
7.00-9.00pm	Step Aerobics	Family Multi-gym	Weight Training	Body Conditioning	

Task 6: Creating a questionnaire

The following document uses a table to set up a simple questionnaire. It is printed in two formats below, one that shows the completed questionnaire and another that demonstrates the way in which a table has been used to create the questionnaire.

You should now be able to set up an appropriate table, apply borders and enter the text without any additional instructions

Chelmer Leisure and Recreation Centre
Staff Workshops in IT

It is planned to run some staff development workshops in IT, during a week in the near future. If you are interested in attending sessions please indicate your area of interest in the following questionnaire.

These sessions could be run in two forms

1. General introduction to software, to introduce IT skills.

2. A more user oriented approach aimed primarily at experimenting with your ideas and to judge how to make use of the facilities available to you.

Please return completed forms to the IT Co-ordinator.

- -

Name:

Please tick those areas of interest

Introducing IT skills

Introducing Windows 3.1 ☐

Introduction to Word Processing using Microsoft Word ☐

Introduction to Graphics using Microsoft Word ☐

Introduction to Spreadsheets using Microsoft Excel ☐

Introduction to Databases using Microsoft Access ☐

Using IT in your area of work

Word Processing ☐

Spreadsheets ☐

Graphics ☐

Please indicate below if you feel that there are any other areas of IT you wish to investigate:-

The version below shows how the table is used in the design of the questionnaire:

Chelmer Leisure and Recreation Centre

Staff Workshops in IT

It is planned to run some staff development workshops in IT, during a week in the near future. If you are interested in attending sessions please indicate you area of interest in the following questionnaire.

These sessions could be run in two forms

1. General introduction to software, to introduce IT skills.

2. A more user oriented approach aimed primarily at experimenting with your ideas and to judge how to make use of the facilities available to you.

Please return completed forms to the IT Co-ordinator.

- -

Name:

Please tick those areas of interest

Introducing IT skills

Introducing Windows 3.1	
Introduction to Word Processing using Microsoft Word	
Introduction to Graphics using Microsoft Word	
Introduction to Spreadsheets using Microsoft Excel	
Introduction to Databases using Microsoft Access	

Using IT in your area of work.

Word Processing	
Spreadsheets	
Graphics	

Please indicate below if you feel that there are any other areas of IT you wish to investigate:-

Large documents (1)

What you will learn in this unit

In this, the first of three units concentrating on larger documents, the tasks concentrate on word processing features that are applicable to documents of more than one page. If the work being produced is for assessment it is often in the form of a report and may be several pages long. Features covered are

■ controlling page breaks

■ numbering pages

■ adding headers and footers.

For most long documents it is useful to know how to add headers, footers and page numbers and to be able to control page breaks.

You may be working on a report and have information in several files. These files can be combined into one file so that, for example, appropriate headers and footers and page numbers may be added. In the following example a large document will be created from smaller documents created in previous tasks.

What you need

To complete this unit you will need

■ the document file **Front** created in Unit 4

■ the document file **Termref** created in Unit 3

■ the document file **Centre** created in Unit 5

■ the document file **Usage** created in Unit 5

■ the document file **Question** created in Unit 10

■ the document file **Findings** created in Unit 4

■ the document file **Summary** created in Unit 4.

Task 1: Combining smaller documents into a larger one

Documents needed for this task are **Front**, **Termref**, **Centre**, **Usage**, **Question**, **Findings** and **Summary**.

1   Open the document file **Front** and, using File-Save As, save this as **Report**.

2   Use *Ctrl/End* to move to the end of the document and press *Enter* to make a new line.

3 Choose **Insert-File** and the **File** dialog box appears.

4 From the list of files select the file **Termref** and click on **OK** .

5 Move to the end of the document.

6 Repeat steps 3-5 to insert each of the document files **Centre**, **Usage**, **Question**, **Findings** and **Summary**.

7 Save this file using **File-Save**.

Pagination and page numbering

As the document being created gets larger Word automatically inserts a page break at the end of each page. Automatic page breaks are called *soft* breaks and are shown in Normal view as a dotted line. As the document is edited and revised Word repositions the page breaks accordingly. This is known as repagination. Repagination occurs whenever you pause during keying. To alter the way in which page breaks occur then manual or *hard* breaks can be inserted.

Adding or removing page breaks

To add a page break, first position the insertion point at the place where the page break is to occur and either

■ use **Insert-Break** and select Page break from the **Break** dialog box

or

■ use the keyboard shortcut, pressing *Ctrl/Enter* simultaneously.

In Normal view a dotted line appears at the point of the page break. In a *hard* break the words Page Break appear in the middle of the line.

A *hard* page break may be selected in the same way as a line of text can be selected, i.e. by positioning the mouse pointer in the left edge of the screen, level with the page break, and clicking. Once selected, the page break can be removed. It is not possible to remove *soft* page breaks; these can controlled either by inserting *hard* page breaks or with paragraph formatting. If possible it is best to avoid *hard* page breaks in a long document as they need to be revised manually whenever the document is revised.

Task 2: Page breaks

1 Open the file **Report** created in Task 1 to insert appropriate page breaks.

2 Position the cursor at the end of the titles and press *Ctrl/Enter*. This should insert a *hard* break at the end of the title page. The body of the report should start on the next page.

3   Repeat this process to put a page break before each heading. You may try adjusting the spacing on the title page to spread out the titles.

4   Use **File-Print Preview** to see how the document looks. Save this document as **Report**.

5   For use in the following tasks, make two copies of this document. Use **File-Save As** and save one copy as **Report1**; repeat and save the second copy as **Report2**. Close all documents.

Page numbering

There are two methods of inserting page numbers.

1   Using **Insert-Page Numbers**. Page numbers may be inserted using **Insert-Page Numbers**. Page numbers may be placed at the bottom of the page (footer) or at the top of the page (header). The alignment of the number can be chosen and whether or not all pages are to be numbered except the first. Remove the ✓ from the **Show number on first page** check box to omit the number from the first page. This is useful for documents that have a title page as the first page.

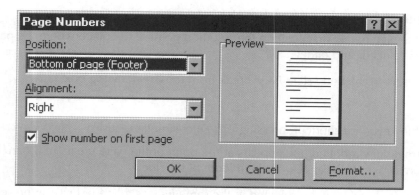

2   As part of a header or footer. This is discussed in the next section.

Task 3: Page numbering

In this task you will apply page numbering to the document **Report1**.

1   Use **Insert-Page Numbers** to add page numbers to the document.

2   Check that position: bottom of page (footer) and alignment: centre are selected.

3   Click on the **Format** button and choose numbering to **start at 0**. This is so that the second page will have a page number of 1.

4   Click on **OK**. Click on **Show number on first page** to remove the tick, to prevent the first page number from displaying. Click on **OK**.

5   Choose **View-Page Layout**. In Page Layout view the page numbers should be visible at the bottom of each page.

6   Use **File-Print Preview** to see the effect.

7   Save the document **Report1**.

If the page numbers are not visible when the document is previewed, then their position in the bottom margin may need adjusting. To do this choose **File-Page Setup** and increase the distance of the header or footer from the edge. You may also need to adjust the position of the top and bottom margins to accommodate the change.

Printing specified pages

In the **Print** dialog box click on the **Pages:** option button. In the associated text box list the page numbers to be printed. For example, to print pages 5, 7 and 9 simply type 5,7,9; to print pages 5 to 8 inclusive type 5-8.

Headers and footers

A header is text or graphics that appears at the top of every page. A footer appears at the bottom of every page. They are useful in long documents as they can be used to indicate, for example, the chapter or section title. In business documents they may contain a reference number or company logo. If the work is an assignment, a header or footer could be used to put the author's name on each page. Word prints headers in the top margin and footers in the bottom margin.

As well as being able to add headers and footers that are the same on every page, Word also offers choices of customising headers and footers.

■ If the document is to be printed on both sides of the paper then headers and footers can be set up so that even numbered pages have one header and odd numbered pages have a different one.

■ If the first page of the document is different from the rest of the document, for example a title page, then headers and footers can be set so that they are different on the first page.

■ If the document is divided into sections then different headers and footers can be applied to each section. Sections are discussed in Unit 14.

Adding or removing a header or footer

To add a header or a footer to your document, use **View-Header and Footer**. The document switches to a page layout view with the text of each page shown in grey (or lighter than normal) and a **Header and Footer** toolbar appears.

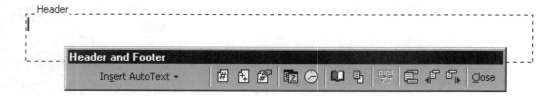

Headers and footers have preset tabs. There is a centre tab in the middle of the page and a right tab at the right edge of the page. By using the preset tabs, the headers or footers will be consistent through the document. Select a suitable font for your header or footer, tab across to the position required and type in the text. Using the buttons, as described following, enter text for headers and footers as required. When finished, click on **Close** .

Icons and buttons in the header and footer toolbar

The first button on the header and footer toolbar allows you to insert AutoText. The next three buttons are

- insert page numbering
- insert number of pages
- format page number.

The next two buttons are

- insert date
- insert time.

To put the date, the time, the page number or the number of pages into a header or footer, position the insertion point and then click on the appropriate icon.

The next two buttons are **Page Setup** and **Show/Hide Document Text** . Clicking on **Page Setup** will display the Page Setup dialog box. Clicking on **Show/Hide Document Text** will toggle between showing or hiding the document text.

The next button is the **Same as Previous** button. Click on the **Same as Previous** button if the header or footer is to be different from the header or footer in the previous section. Unit 14 discusses dividing the document up into sections.

The first button of the final group of three allows you to switch between the header and footer. The next two buttons allow forward and backward movement between different headers or footers. There will only be different headers and footers, if Different first page, or Different odd and even, in Page Setup, have been selected or if there are different sections in the document.

When the text for the header or footer has been typed in click on the **Close** button to return to the document text body.

Before printing it is a good idea to preview the document. Headers and footers can be positioned by choosing **File-Page Setup** and defining their required position in the From edge section of the **Page Setup-Margins** dialog box.

Page numbering in headers or footers

By clicking on the **Page Number Format** button in the Header and Footer toolbar or through using **Insert-Page Numbers** and clicking on the **Format** button, page numbering can be controlled. The **Page Numbers Format** dialog box will be displayed.

The format of page numbering may be chosen from the **Number Format:** box, i.e. Arabic or Roman numerals or alphabetic numbering. This can be done by opening the **Number Format:** list box. It is also possible to alter the number at which page numbering starts. This can be useful if the document is long and is stored as separate files. The start page number of the second and subsequent files may be altered accordingly. Different formats of page numbering may be used in different sections of a document.

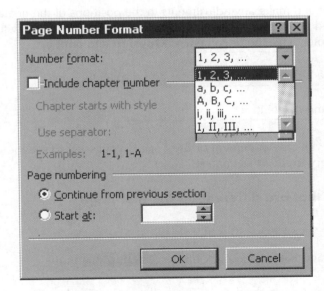

Editing or removing existing headers and footers

To remove or edit an existing header or footer:

1   Use **View-Header and Footer** and display either the Header or Footer using the **Switch between Header and Footer** button.

2   Edit the text in the header or footer in the normal fashion. Text may be pasted into the header or footer, or copied from it. To remove the header or footer, simply delete all the text.

3   Click on **Close**.

Task 4: Headers and footers

In this task a header and a footer are added to the document **Qdesign**. Open the document.

1 Choose **View-Header and Footer** and the insertion point is ready positioned in the header.

2 Press the *Tab* key to move to the centre tab and type in the text Adjusting Margins.

3 Click on the **Switch between Header and Footer** button to display the footer.

4 Press the *Tab* key twice to move to the right tab and type in your name.

5 Click on **Close** .

6 Preview the document and make any adjustments to the positions of the header and footer as described above. Also view the document in page layout view to see the header and footer. Save the document as **Qdesign** and print it.

7 From Normal view use **View-Header and Footer** and display the footer.

8 Select the footer text and delete it.

9 Click on **Close** . Preview the document or use Page Layout view to see the effect. It is not necessary to save this change.

Headers and footers that are different on the first page

To select this option:

1 Choose **View-Header and Footer** and click on the **Page Setup** button.

2 Click in the **Different first page** check box. This will create a **first header** and a **first footer** as well as the normal **header** and **footer**. The text in a First Header may be different from the Header and the text in a First Footer may be different from the Footer.

3 Use the **Switch between Header and Footer** button and the **Show Next** and **Show Previous** buttons to navigate to the header or footer desired and key in the text.

4 Click on **Close** .

Task 5: Making headers and footers different on the first page

Using the document **Report2**, this task adds a header and a footer both of which will not appear on the first page of the document. Page numbering is incorporated into the footer.

1 Use the **Page Number Format** dialog box available through **Insert-Page Numbers** to start the page numbering at 0 so that the first page of text will appear to be page 1. Click on **OK** and **Close**.

2 Choose **View-Header and Footer**.

3 Click on the **Page Setup** button and click in the **Different first page** check box.

4 Move to the header (use the **Show Next** button to move to Header from First Header).

5 Key in the text 'Fitness Suite Feasibility Study'.

6 Move to the footer (not the First Footer).

7 Press the *Tab* key once and click on the page numbering icon.

8 Press *Tab* again and key in your name.

9 Click on **Close**.

10 Save the document **Report2**.

At this point review and compare the documents **Report1** and **Report2**. If you wish, make extra copies of the document **Report** and experiment with headers and footers.

Odd and even headers and footers

Odd and even headers and footers are used when the finished document will be printed like a book where both sides of the paper are printed on. In a book left-hand pages are even numbered and right-hand pages are odd numbered. A header or footer can be defined so that it reads across from an even to an odd page. Different information about the document can appear on odd and even pages, for example chapter title on even pages and section title on odd pages. To achieve this

1 Choose **View-Header and Footer** and click on the **Page Setup** button.

2   Click on the **Different odd and even** check box. This will create an Even Header, an Odd Header, an Even Footer, and an Odd Footer. The text in the Even Header may be different from the Odd Header and the text in the Even Footer may be different from the Odd Footer.

3   Use the **Switch between Header and Footer** button and the **Show Next** and **Show Previous** buttons to navigate to the header or footer desired and key in the text.

4   Click on **Close** .

Note that the odd and even headers/footers option may be used in conjunction with the different first page option.

Footnotes and endnotes

Footnotes and endnotes are notes of reference, explanation or comment. A word in the main text can be marked with a footnote or endnote reference mark. A number is commonly used for a reference mark. Footnotes are found at the bottom of the page and endnotes are found at the end of the document. Word allows footnotes and endnotes of any length to be added to a document.

Text used in a footnote can be formatted just as any other text. To add a footnote or endnote:

1   In Normal view, first position the insertion point at the end of the word that the footnote or endnote is to refer to.

2   Use **Insert-Footnote** and the **Footnote and Endnote** dialog box appears.

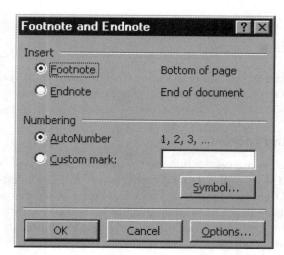

3   Click on **OK** and a footnote pane appears as shown below. A reference mark is positioned in the document at the position of the insertion point.

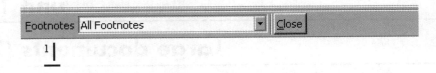

4 Key in the text. The insertion point is ready positioned following the reference mark.

5 Click on **Close** .

As footnotes or endnotes are added Word automatically numbers them. Word will automatically renumber footnote/endnote and reference marks whenever footnotes/endnotes are added, deleted or moved.

Large documents (2)

What you will learn in this unit

In this unit the activities continue work on word processing features that are applicable to documents of more than one page. Features covered are

- paragraph formatting
- styles.

In Units 5, 6 and 7 formatting that can be applied to paragraphs has been investigated. In this unit formatting that can be applied when creating a long document will be considered. By altering paragraph formatting the position of page breaks can be controlled. Using styles allows you to be consistent in your work in terms of the format of headings and sub-headings and the body of your text.

What you need

To complete this unit you will need

- the document file **Qdesign** created in Unit 3
- the document file **Report** created in Unit 12
- the document file **Front** created in Unit 4.

Paragraph formatting

In many documents paragraphs have space between them. This unit is an example. Instead of pressing _Enter_ to create a blank line between paragraphs Word allows you to define the amount of space before and after a paragraph. Use **Format-Paragraph** to display the **Paragraph** dialog box with the **Indents and Spacing** tab selected. In the spacing section the values in the **Before:** and **After:** boxes can be adjusted. Spacing is altered in increments of 6 points, which can be considered to be half a line. Note that if you have space after a paragraph and the following paragraph has space before it then the space between the paragraphs will be the sum of the before and after spacing.

Other paragraphs may require different spacing, for example headings or tables, and these can be easily adjusted from the **Paragraph** dialog box.

Task 1: Controlling space between paragraphs

This task experiments with altering the spacing between paragraphs. Open the document **Qdesign**.

1   If you have blank lines in between paragraphs, remove them. Click on the
    Show/Hide ¶ button to show the paragraph marks.

2   Position the insertion point in the first paragraph.

3   Choose **Format-Paragraph**, and select the **Indents and spacing** tab. Set the
    spacing before to 12 points (one line).

4   Position the insertion point in the second paragraph.

5   Choose **Format-Paragraph** and set the **spacing before** to 24 points (two lines).

6   Position the insertion point in the third paragraph.

7   Choose **Format-Paragraph** and set the **spacing after** to 24 points (two lines).

8   Save and print this document.

9   Experiment with setting the line spacing before and after the paragraphs in this
    document.

Controlling page breaks using paragraph formatting

Page breaks are controlled through the pagination section of the **Format-Paragraph-Line and Page Breaks** dialog box. There are three types of formatting available.

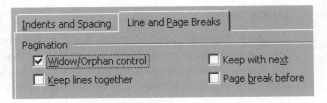

- **Keep lines together**: use this to prevent a page break within a paragraph. Word
  normally exercises widow and orphan control, if the **Widow/Orphan control** box
  is checked; that is to say, it will prevent widows and orphans from occurring. A
  widow is a single line at the beginning of a paragraph left at the bottom of a page
  and an orphan is a single line at the end of a paragraph at the top of a page.

- **Keep with next**: use this to prevent a page break occurring between the paragraph
  and the following one, for example, to keep a sub-heading with its following paragraph or to keep the lines of a table together.

- **Page break before**: if a paragraph such as a heading is formatted with this, then a
  page break will be inserted before the paragraph. If each chapter of your document is to appear on a new page then format the chapter heading with **Page break
  before** by clicking in the appropriate check box. To remove this page break the
  formatting must be removed from the paragraph.

By making use of these formatting options the need for *hard* pages breaks to be
inserted in a long document can be eliminated. When the document is altered the

page breaks will follow the rules applied in the paragraph formatting and conse-
quently should occur in sensible places.

Task 2: Using soft breaks

The *hard* breaks originally put into the document **Report** are to be replaced by *soft*
breaks controlled by the type of paragraph formatting.

1 Open the document **Report**.

2 Remove the hard page break at the end of the title page by selecting it and pressing the *Delete* key.

3 Position the insertion point in the heading 'Terms of Reference'.

4 Use **Format-Paragraph** and click on the **Page break before** check box. Click on
   OK. In normal view you should see a soft break inserted. Switch to page layout view or use **File-Print Preview** to verify the effect.

5 Replace all of the remaining *hard* breaks with *soft* breaks. Remove each one and
   format the heading paragraph using **Page break before**.

6 Save the document **Report**.

Using styles

A style is the name applied to the 'look' of the text in a document. The look of the
text depends upon the formatting instructions that have been applied to it. A heading is usually made to look different from the body of the text, i.e. it has a different
style. In a document there may be different levels of headings, for example chapter
or section headings, and within these are sub-headings. Word has the facility for different styles to be created and stored under different names. Different styles can be
used for different headings.

Various formatting may be applied to create a style

1 Character formatting such as

   ■ typeface

   ■ size

   ■ bold, italics or underlining

   ■ special effects such as shadow or outline.

2 Paragraph formatting such as

   ■ alignment

   ■ spacing

- margins
- pagination.

3 Layout formatting such as

- tabs
- bullets and numbering
- borders and shading.

4 Language formatting: if text is written in a different language then Word will know to use the appropriate dictionary (if available) when spell checking.

Selecting a style

Word comes with some predefined styles and these can be listed by opening the style list box at the leftmost end of the formatting toolbar.

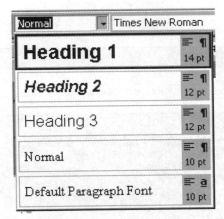

To select a style:

1 position the insertion point, either to key in some new text or in an existing paragraph. If you wish to alter the style of a portion of the document which is more than one paragraph long, then select the required portion

2 open the **Style** list box and highlight the required style

3 either key in text which will have the selected style, or the chosen paragraph or portion will be changed into the new style.

To see the definition of a style position the insertion point in some text that uses the style, say Normal, and choose **Format-Style**. In the **Style** dialog box a description of the style is given.

Styles may be used as the document is being keyed in or they can be applied after the text has been keyed in. The real advantage in using styles is in being able to define custom styles. Should an alteration in the style be desirable then by changing the definition of the style, all parts of the document that use that style will be altered accordingly. This makes it easier to produce consistent documents.

Defining a custom style

New styles can be defined, or existing ones modified using **Format-Style**. Consider defining the style for the main body of the text in the document.

1 Position the insertion point in a paragraph that is to take the main body style, or position it on a new line.

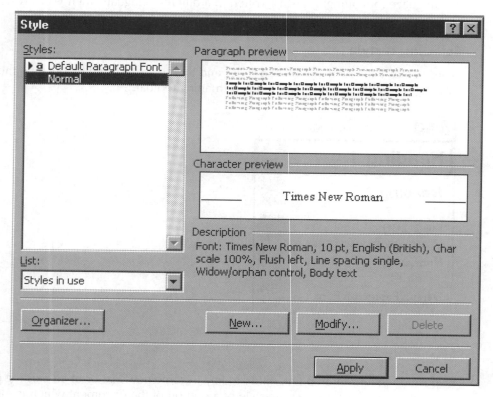

2 Use **Format-Style** to display the **Style** dialog box.

3 Click on the **New** button and the **New Style** dialog box appears (see below). In the **Name** box type in the name for the new style, e.g. Text body.

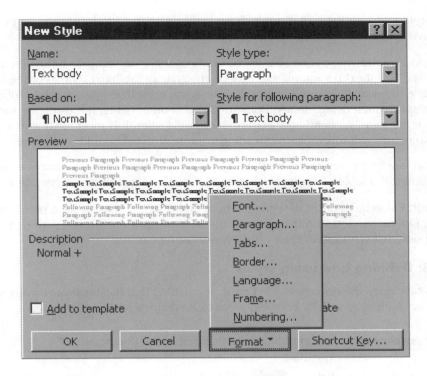

4 Select the appropriate formatting by clicking on the **Format** button and choosing from the list:

- ■ **Font** produces **Font** dialog box

- ■ **Paragraph** produces **Paragraph** dialog box

- ■ **Tabs** produces **Tabs** dialog box

- ■ **Border** produces **Borders and Shading** dialog box

- ■ **Language** produces **Language** dialog box

- ■ **Frame** produces **Frame** dialog box

- ■ **Numbering** produces **Bullets and Numbering** dialog box.

5 Make required choices from these dialog boxes.

6 Choose the **Style for the following paragraph:** from the list box. In this case it would be Text body. Click on **OK**.

7 When the style is defined click on **Apply**. The defined style name will be available through the style list box.

At the top of the dialog box there are two list boxes, a **Based on:** box and a **Style for the following paragraph:** box. By basing your custom styles on one particular style formatting changes can be made easier. If all the styles are based on a style that has a Times New Roman font and a decision is made to change to Arial then by altering the font upon which the others are all based will cause them to be altered unless they have specific character formatting applied.

The **Style for following paragraph:** list box defines the style that is to follow the one being used. The next paragraph will take on the style of the 'next style'. For the text body style the next style should be **text body** as the most likely paragraph to follow a paragraph written using the text body format is another paragraph using the same format. If the style is a heading style, e.g. **Heading 1**, then it is most likely that a text body paragraph will follow so for Heading 1 the next style should be **text body**.

Note that heading styles (there are 9, Heading 1 to Heading 9) should only be used for headings. If a table of contents is required Word uses headings to generate it.

It is worth the extra effort in designing various styles to give your work a professional look. Do not use lots of different fonts; the best effects are achieved with one font used in different sizes rather than with a variety of typefonts.

Task 3: Defining and using styles

For this task open the document file **Front**. Formatting that has been previously set up can be defined as a style. Four styles are to be defined for this title page.

1   First position the insertion point in the first line of the title page.

2   Use **Format-Style**, click on **New** and in the **Name:** box type in the name Title1.

3   Click on **OK** and then on the **Apply** button.

4   Select the second line, open the style list box and select **Title1**. Nothing appears to happen except that the style of Title1 has been applied to that paragraph.

5   Position the insertion point in the author name. As above, create a style called **Title4**.

6   Apply this style to the last four lines of the page. You may need to click on the **Format** button in the **Style** dialog box and choose **Paragraph** to remove spacing before/after a paragraph.

7   In a similar manner define and apply suitable styles, **Title2** and **Title3**, to the second and third portions of the page. Hint: keep paragraph spacing to zero; add spacing to the first line of a portion after the styles have been defined.

8   Save the document as **Front**.

Task 4: Modifying a style

You may change your mind about the styles which you have chosen and wish to make changes.

Using the document file **Front** make changes to the styles created in Task 3.

1   Position the insertion point in text which has the style **Title1** applied to it.

2   Choose **Format-tyle** and click on Modify . Click on Format , choose **Font** and select a different font. Click on OK .

3   Click on OK in the **Modify Style** dialog box and click on Apply . All text throughout the document defined with this style will take on these new properties.

4   Experiment with the other styles. Changes to their fonts, sizes, margins and alignment can be made. If you prefer the styles you have chosen save the document.

Task 5: Storing styles in templates

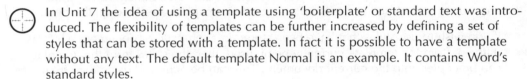

In Unit 7 the idea of using a template using 'boilerplate' or standard text was introduced. The flexibility of templates can be further increased by defining a set of styles that can be stored with a template. In fact it is possible to have a template without any text. The default template Normal is an example. It contains Word's standard styles.

The styles defined for the title page could also be used for title pages of other pieces of work. These styles can be saved as a template which can be applied to future documents. This task uses a straightforward method for setting up a style template.

1   Open a new document using **File-New**.

2   Select the Template option button.

3   Choose Blank Document from the list of templates as the new template is to be based on this template. Click on OK .

4   Type the word Title1 with your preferred formatting and set up the style **Title1** as described in Task 3.

5   Repeat for each style, i.e. on the next line type Title2 and set up the style **Title2** etc.

6   Use **File-Save As** and type Titles in the filename box. This file is saved as a .dot template file. Close the file using **File-Close**.

7   To use this template, start a new document using **File-New** and select **Titles** from the list of templates. Replace the words Title1, Title2 etc. with the desired titles. It is not necessary to use all of the styles each time a front page is created. Save the new title page in the usual manner.

You can combine text and style in a template, for example, the name of the institution could be used instead of Title1. You could remove the text in the template before saving, i.e. before the last step above, to leave just the style definitions in the template.

Adding styles to a template

As a document is created styles may be defined which would be useful to be stored. These may be added to the document template by clicking in the **Add to template** check box in the bottom left-hand corner of the New Style or Modify Style dialog box. When you save your document Word will ask if you wish to save the changes to the template.

Task 6: Copying styles

If you wish new styles to be added to the template file, or copied from one document to another, then this can be done using the **Organizer** dialog box. In the list on the left of the dialog box the styles used in the active document or its template are shown. Styles used in the Normal document template are listed on the right.

If you wish to use styles that have been stored in a template or document which is different from the template currently being used, then the styles from that template can be copied into the current document. This can be achieved using the **Organizer** dialog box.

In this task the styles created and saved in the template Titles.dot are to be merged into the document **Report**.

1 Open the document file **Report**.

2 Use **Format-Style** and click on **Organizer**.

3 Click on **Close File** on the right side of the dialog box. Next click on **Open File** and select the template Titles.dot.

Note: You may select either a document or a template from which to copy styles. The **Open** dialog box allows you to change drive or directory; or to list document or template files.

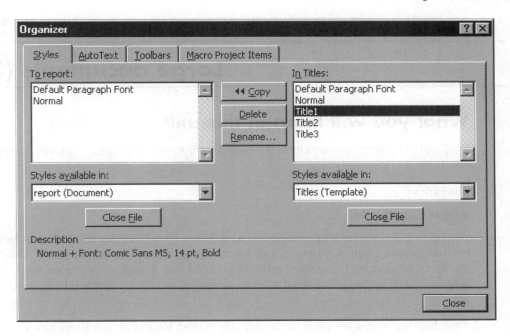

4 Select **Title1** from the list of style names and click on `<< Copy`. Repeat for other styles in this document which you may wish to copy.

5 Click on `Close`.

6 Open the `Style` list box (on the formatting toolbar) and you should find that the styles you copied are listed.

7 Apply these to the title page. Select each portion of the title page in turn, open the style list box and choose the appropriate style.

8 Save the document **Report**.

Large documents (3)

What you will learn in this unit

This unit completes the activities associated with long documents. Features covered are

■ sections

■ contents and index.

By dividing a document up into sections, different formatting such as different headers and footers, page numbering and orientation or layout can be achieved. A document can be divided into any number of sections and a section can be of any length. A section can be as short as one paragraph or as long as the whole document.

If the heading styles are used in the document then Word can use these to create a table of contents for the long document.

Dividing the document into sections

You may divide a document into sections after you have keyed in all the text or you can create sections as you work. If this is new to you then it is advisable to perform this activity when the text of the document is complete. To put a section break into a document use **Insert-Break** and from the following dialog box select a section break from the choices available.

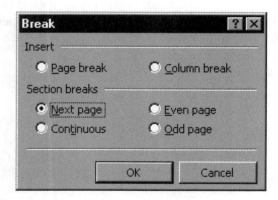

■ A section break may be chosen so that it starts on the next page, or so that there is no apparent break. This is the **Continuous** option.

■ To start a new section on the next page select the **Next page** option.

■ If the document is to be printed on both sides of the page then it may be desirable to start a new section on either the next odd or even page. This choice can be made by clicking on the appropriate option button.

Word separates each section with a section break, which appears in Normal view as a double dotted line across the screen with text describing the type of break, for example 'End of Section (Next Page)', in its centre. A new section should be created when a change occurs in the document. For example

- the number of newspaper-style columns on a page. Here a continuous section break should be used

- the alignment of the text, portrait or landscape. Here a next page section break should be used

- the format, sequence and position of page numbering

- the text and formatting of headers and footers.

Applying different formatting to individual sections

Once the document has been divided up into sections then different formatting may be applied.

Headers and footers

Using **View-Header and Footer** and the **Page Setup** button you can specify the types of headers and footers required in each section of your document. If the header or footer is the same as that in the previous section then click on the **Same as Previous** button. Two headers are illustrated below. The header area is enclosed by a dashed bounding rectangle with information about the type of header, the section number and whether it is the same as the previous header.

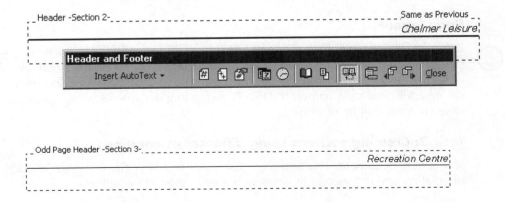

Footers are shown in a similar way.

Task 1: Creating sections and applying different headers and footers

This task shows how different headers and footers may be applied to different sections of a document. Open the document **Report**, created in Unit 12.

1 Position the insertion point at the left of the F of the heading 'Findings from market research'.

2 Choose Insert-Break.

3 Click on Next page. A double dotted line with the text Section Break (Next Page) appears on the screen above the heading.

4 Use View-Header and Footer, click on the ` Page Setup ` button and check that Different first page does *not* have a tick in its box. Click on ` OK `.

5 In the Header - Section 2 area overwrite any existing heading with the text Findings. Click on ` Close `.

6 Save the document as **Report**. Use File-Print Preview in two pages mode to view the document. Print out the last two pages.

Page numbering

Each section may have its own page numbering. To customise a section make sure the insertion point is in the section to be customised. Use Insert-Page Numbers and alter the page numbering through the Page Numbers dialog box.

Page layout

Different sections may have different formatting; for example the orientation, page size or the number of columns can alter. Note that styles remain the same regardless of section breaks. If you want to use different fonts in a particular section then define additional style names. In Unit 21 formatting documents with newspaper style columns will be discussed.

Task 2: Creating sections using different orientations

Start a new document. This two-page document will have the first page in portrait orientation and the second in landscape. Key in the following text.

1 Press *Enter* to make a new line and use Insert-Break to insert a section break starting on the next page.

2 Select landscape orientation using File-Page Setup, click on the ` Paper Size ` tab and in the orientation section click on landscape.

> CHELMER LEISURE AND RECREATION CENTRE
>
> ## MEMORANDUM
>
> To: All Multi-gym Staff   Date: 8 October 199X
>
> From: Geoff Richards
>
> MULTI-GYM ACTIVITY PROGRAMME
>
> Further to last Wednesday's meeting I have completed the activity timetable for the multi-gym. A copy is attached to this memo. Thank you for your hard work and co-operation in devising activity programmes to be used in the multi-gym.

3 Using Insert-File insert the document **Timetble** created in Unit 11. Adjust the table to fill the page. Note that you will need to scroll left and right to view the width of the page, or use the zoom facility to 'shrink' the view.

4 View the document using **File-Print Preview** in **two pages** mode. The first page should be displayed in portrait orientation and the second in landscape. Print out the document.

Creating a simple table of contents

Most large documents have headings. Some headings are more important than others; for example a chapter heading is more important than a paragraph heading. Word allows nine heading styles to be defined. Heading 1 is the most important and Heading 9 is the least important. Usually two or three heading styles are enough for a document.

By defining and using the heading styles for your documents, not only is consistency maintained but Word is also able to use them to create a table of contents. This is best illustrated in the following task.

Task 3: Creating a table of contents

A simple table of contents is to be created for the document **Report**.

1 Open the document **Report**.

2 Choose and define a style for Heading 1.

3 Apply this style to the heading at the top of each page.

4 Save the document.

5   Position the insertion point where the table of contents is to go. Tables of contents may be put anywhere, but it is advisable to choose the end of the document. By putting a page break at the end of the document and inserting the table of contents after it, page numbering is unaffected.

6   Use *Ctrl/End* to move to the end of the document. Insert a page break or better still key in Contents and format this with page break before.

7   Position the cursor under Contents and choose **Insert-Index and Tables** and click on the **Table of Contents** tab.

8   Select a format for the table of contents and click on **OK**. The table of contents will be inserted.

9   Save the document as **Report**. Should the document be revised the table of contents can be updated by positioning the insertion point in the table of contents and pressing *F9*. You will be given the choice of updating either just the page numbers or the whole table of contents.

Note: You can use a table of contents to 'jump' to a specific heading in your document, by double clicking on the page number of the heading you wish to go to.

Basics of creating a chart

What you will learn in this unit

This unit covers the basic functions necessary to create and save charts. Later units explore the variety of different ways in which you can format charts. At the end of this unit you will be able to

■ start Word's charting facility, Microsoft Graph

■ enter data into a datasheet

■ create a chart

■ embed a chart into a Word document

■ create two or more copies of a chart

■ edit a chart

■ print a chart.

This unit shows you how to create a simple graph and insert it into a Word document.

Microsoft Graph

To enter Graph, with a Word document open, choose **Insert-Object-Microsoft Graph 97 Chart** or click the **Insert Chart** button on the toolbar. If this button is not shown on your toolbar then you may add it (see Customising toolbars in Quick Reference 3). The screen will display a linked datasheet and chart which may show the default chart. Data entered on the datasheet will be displayed on the chart.

The Datasheet window

Document1 - Datasheet		A	B	C	D	E
		1st Qtr	2nd Qtr	3rd Qtr	4th Qtr	
1	East	20.4	27.4	90	20.4	
2	West	30.6	38.6	34.6	31.6	
3	North	45.9	46.9	45	43.9	
4						

The Datasheet window is like a simple spreadsheet worksheet. Labels for data are entered in the first row and column of the data sheet. Do not type data in these cells. This first row and column remain visible as you scroll the sheet. Various parts of the datasheet have names that we will use later. The important components of the datasheet are listed in the following table.

Component	Description
Row and column headings	Above the first row and to the left of the first column of the datasheet
Cell	One rectangle of the datasheet
Active cell	Currently selected cell
Data point	Single cell value
data series	A row or column of data used to plot one set of bars, columns, one line, or one pie.
Series names	Names that identify each row and column of data
Tick mark labels	When the data series are in rows, the tick mark labels are the column labels. When data series are in columns, the tick mark labels are the row labels.

The chart

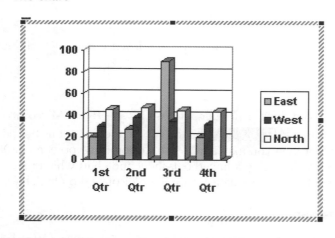

The data in the form of a chart appears in the document. Again, parts of the window have names that will be used later. The important components of the chart window are listed in the following table.

Component	Description
Chart	The entire area inside the chart window
Data marker	A bar, shape or dot that marks a single data point or value
Data series	A group of related data points

Component	Description
Axis	A line that serves as a reference for plotting data on a chart
Tick mark	A small line that intersects the axis and marks off a category
Plot area	The area in which Graph plots the data
Gridlines	Lines that extend from the tick marks across the chart
Chart text	Text that describes data or items in a chart
Legend	The key

Managing Datasheet window and chart

All of the operations that can normally be performed on windows can be performed on the Datasheet window. It can be sized by moving its borders, or moved by dragging the title bar to a new position.

To switch between windows click on the one that you wish to be active. If you would like to remove the Datasheet window, click on **View-Datasheet**. The Datasheet can be recalled by applying **View-Datasheet** again. Alternatively, click on the **View-Datasheet** button on the toolbar.

Creating a simple chart

To create a simple chart you merely need to enter data into the datasheet. If you already have the default data and chart on your screen, you will first need to clear the default data. This can be achieved by

- selecting the datasheet, by clicking in the top left-hand box. The datasheet should be highlighted in black

- pressing the *Delete* key

- clicking on any datasheet cell to clear the highlight.

Once you have an empty datasheet and chart you are ready to begin. Enter labels in the first row and first column and data in the remaining cells. Move from one cell to the next by using the *Tab* or *right arrow* key. To move backwards from one cell to another use *Shift/Tab* or the *left arrow* key. Use the up and down arrow keys to move the active cell up or down. You may also use the mouse pointer to position the active cell by pointing and clicking.

Inserting a chart into a document

To insert a chart into a document, simply click on the document outside the chart. The hatching border will disappear. Once in the document the chart may be selected and manipulated with any of the operations that can be applied to any other 'floating' object, such as moving, copying, cutting, pasting and sizing. If you do not want the chart to 'float' (and note that floating objects do not appear in Normal view) then with the chart selected use **Format-Object**, choose the **Position** tab and remove the tick from the **Float over text** check box.

Saving a chart

Charts are saved as part of the document in which they are embedded. To save a chart place the chart in a document and save the document in the normal way using **File-Save**. Note that the chart, the data and all formats are saved as part of your document.

Printing a chart

Charts are also printed as part of the document in which they are embedded. Print the document in the normal way using **File-Print Preview** to view the document first, and then click on the **Print** button.

Editing a chart

To edit a chart

■ double click on the chart in your document

■ make whatever changes you wish to the chart or the data

■ when finished click on the main document and save, as described previously.

Task 1: Creating a chart of one data series

We wish to create a simple chart showing one data series, as shown below. This chart shows the use of the multi-gym by different categories of users during the week ending 5/07/97.

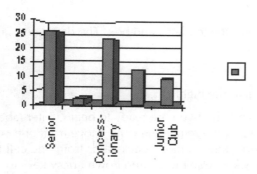

1 Choose **Insert-Object Microsoft Graph97 Chart**, or click on ▥ to enter Graph. The default datasheet and chart should be displayed.

2 If necessary clear the default chart as indicated above.

3 Enter the following data in the second row in the chart with the labels in the first row, leaving the first column blank.

Senior	Junior	Concessionary	Senior Club	Junior Club
26	2	23	12	9

4 Note that at this point we can not see the full labels in the first row.

5 Click on the Chart window to examine your chart. Although it may not be exactly like the one illustrated, it will lack a title and axes labels and would benefit from further formatting. We will attend to this later.

6 Insert your chart in your document by clicking outside it.

7 Save the document, with its embedded chart using the filename **Users**, by choosing **File-Save**.

Creating two or more copies of a chart

Once you have inserted a chart into a document you may create an additional copy by cutting and pasting.

■ Select chart.

■ Choose **Edit-Copy**.

■ Move the insertion point to where you wish to insert the second copy of the chart in your document.

■ Choose **Edit-Paste**.

This operation can also be used to transfer charts between documents, if you have two or more documents open in separate windows.

A copy of the chart may be edited as indicated above and used to create another chart based on the same or related data. Thus several different displays can be created showing the same or different subsets of the same data series.

Task 2 Creating a chart with two data series

The objective of this task is to create two copies of a chart, and then to reformat the second chart.

1 Select your chart in your document **Users** by clicking on it.

2 Make a second copy using **Edit-Copy**, move the cursor to the position for the second copy and use **Edit-Paste**.

3 Double click on the second copy to enter Graph. If the Datasheet window is not active then click on it.

4 Add the following data in the next row of the datasheet.

42	3	31	6	9

5 Examine the new chart. Two data series should now be displayed as below. Drag the sizing handle of the chart to make it fit across the width of the page.

6 Update the chart in the document. Do not worry if your chart does not look exactly like the one illustrated; chart formatting will be discussed in Unit 17. Note that you now have two versions of your chart in your document. Save the document again as **Users**.

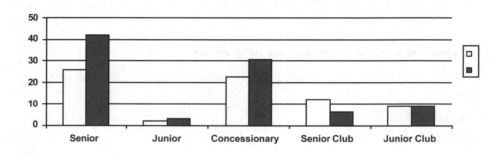

Working with the datasheet

What you will learn in this unit

The datasheet is like a simple worksheet in a spreadsheet package. You will need to be able to move around the datasheet, edit the values in cells, define the data series to be displayed, change column widths, clear, move and copy data, and insert and delete rows and columns.

The data to be displayed in the chart is entered in the datasheet. By entering text in the top row and the first column it is possible to add labels to the chart. In addition, formatting data on the datasheet can affect the formatting of data elsewhere. By the end of this unit you will be able to

- move around the datasheet
- edit the values in cells
- change column widths
- clear, move and copy data, and insert and delete rows and columns
- define the data series to be displayed.

What you need

To complete this unit you will need:

- the document file **Users** created in Unit 15.

The following table summarises some of the key datasheet operations.

To	Do this
Selection	
Select a cell	Click on the cell
Select a range of cells	Point to the first cell, and drag through the remaining cells
Select a row or column	Click on the grey box at the side of a row or at the top of a column
Select entire datasheet	Click on grey box in upper left corner of the datasheet
Entering and editing data	
Enter data	Select cell, type data and press *Enter*
Edit data	Double click on cells so that the insertion point appears in the cell. Position insertion point and edit

To	Do this
Clear cell contents	Select cells. Either press the _Delete_ key or choose Edit-Clear. Decide whether you wish to clear all, formats or contents
Undoing changes	Choose Edit-Undo
Managing columns and rows	
Change column widths	Move the pointer onto the top of the column boundary until it appears as a double headed arrow. Drag the line to the right of the desired column heading to give the desired width
Insert a row or column	Select row or columns where the new row or column is to go. Choose Insert-Cells
Delete a row or column	Select the row or column to be deleted. Choose Edit-Delete
Moving and copying data	
Move data	Select cells. Choose Edit-Cut. Select upper left cell of paste area. Choose Edit-Paste
Copy data	Select cells. Choose Edit-Copy. Select upper left cell of paste area. Choose Edit-Paste

Task 1: Formatting and editing a datasheet

Using the second chart in the document **Users**, we wish to improve the format of the datasheet so that it appears similar to the one displayed below. Here are some functions to try.

1 Widen the columns so that the labels in the first row can be displayed clearly, by placing the pointer on the column boundary and dragging the column line to the right of the desired column heading to give an appropriate width.

2 Enter the following dates in the first column against the respective rows of data: 12/07/9x, and 19/07/9x (enter whichever final digit is appropriate for the year in which you are working).

3 Enter additional data for the following three weeks in the next three rows, as shown.

06/12/9X	40	9	14	13	4
07/02/9X	39	12	15	6	7
23/09/9X	56	5	16	8	6

4   Insert a new column between the Junior Club and Senior Club columns to accommodate the following data by clicking on the Junior Club heading cell and using **Insert-Cells**.

Youth Club	0	4	8	10	21

Widen the column as necessary to accommodate the heading.

5   Move the column with Junior Club heading next to the column with Junior as a heading, by first making a blank column in the appropriate place. Click on the heading cell at the top of the Concessionary column and choose **Insert-Cells**. Select the cells in the Junior Club column, and then put them on the clipboard using **Edit-Cut**. Next click on the top cell in the new empty column and choose **Edit-Paste**.

6   Move the Senior Club column adjacent to the Senior column in a similar way.

7   Your datasheet should now show the following data.

	Senior	Senior Club	Junior	Junior Club	Concessionary	Youth Club
19/4/9x	26	12	2	9	23	0
16/8/9x	42	6	3	9	31	4
6/12/9x	40	13	9	4	15	8
7/2/9y	39	6	12	7	16	10
23/9/9y	56	8	5	6	19	21

8   Examine your chart. It is now attempting to display too much data and does not look very effective. We would like to choose which data to display. For now, simply click in your document, and save it again as **Users**.

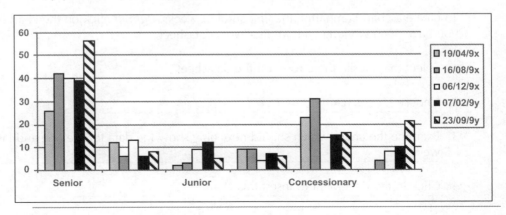

121

Determining which data is displayed on the chart

In your first chart design you will have accepted the default arrangement, which is that all data on the datasheet is displayed on the chart, and each row is regarded as one data series. Often you may wish to be more selective and display only some of the data in one chart, and other data on a later chart (see the section on creating two copies of a charts in Unit 15). Two commands are useful in this context.

- Data: the Data menu offers the opportunity to define which sets of data should by displayed as a data series. Two important options that are self-explanatory are **Data-Series in Columns** and **Data-Series in Rows**

- **Excluding and including data**: these options control the data that will appear on the chart, so that data may remain on the datasheet but need not appear on the chart. To exclude data select a row or column. Choose **Data-Exclude Row/Col**. Note that the excluded data row or column is no longer displayed on the chart, and appears dimmed on the datasheet and that the heading cell for excluded columns or rows loses its 'button-like' appearance.

A quicker method of excluding is to double click the row heading to the left of the row or the column heading above the column.

Once excluded, rows or columns can be included again by a similar process.

Task 2: Creating a series of charts from a single chart

This task again uses the chart and datasheet that you have embedded in the document saved as **Users**. Open the document and click on the last graph with which you were working. We observed at the end of Task 1 that the chart was currently showing too many data series to be effective, so we would like to be more selective and create a series of charts that show selected data series. Suppose, for example, that we wish to compare the attendance data for the first and last weeks shown. Alternatively we might like to compare Junior Club data with Junior data. We will create two charts to display such data.

To create a chart comparing the first and last weeks, double click on the chart that you have been working with to display its datasheet.

1   Select the middle three rows on the datasheet.

2   Choose **Data-Exclude Row/Col**.

3   Examine the chart, which should now only show the data for the first and last weeks.

4   Click in the document to insert this chart.

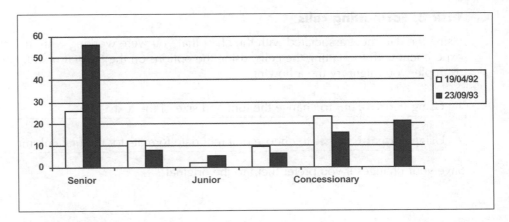

Now we wish to create a chart comparing Junior and Junior club data.

5   To create other charts based on the same datasheet, create an additional copy of the chart as in Unit 15 using **Edit-Copy** and **Edit-Paste**.

6   Double-click on the new copy of the chart to enter Graph again and click on the **View Datasheet** icon to display the datasheet once more.

7   Include the excluded rows, using **Data-Exclude Row/Col**.

8   Exclude all columns that you do not wish to display in this chart using **Data-Exclude Row/Col**.

9   Examine the chart, which should now simply compare the data for Juniors with that for the Junior Club, but you should see that it needs rearranging.

10 Click on the **By Column** button ⊞ in the toolbar for a more acceptable display. Examine the new chart.

11 Insert this chart in the document. Save the document as **Users**.

Formatting cells

The appearance of cells in the datasheet can be changed by modifying font, size, style and the colour of data in a cell. There are a number of numerical formats that can be adopted, for example, currency signs, different numbers of decimal places and thousands separators. Numerical values next to tick marks can be changed by defining or changing the number format of the cell in the second column of the second row of the datasheet. All of the formatting options are shown on the **Format** menu.

Task 3: Formatting cells

Using the datasheet associated with the chart that you were working with in Task 2, experiment with formatting the cells, using the options on the **Format** menu. For example, you might try the following.

1   Using **Format-Font** to change the font and size of the text.

2   Using **Format-Number** to choose different date formats for the first column.

Save your changes if you prefer them to the original.

Changing chart type, format and text

What you will learn in this unit

Graph offers a number of different means for formatting charts. This unit starts to explore some of the options by indicating possible chart types and formatting options. Charts need to be clearly labelled. Some text is placed on the chart by Graph. We may wish to delete, or edit, this text, and add other text. Typically text on a chart includes chart titles, axes labels, data marker labels and other text. Text can be attached or unattached. Typical attached text includes chart titles, axes labels and data marker labels. Unattached text may be moved freely to any position on the chart.

Other features of charts that can be manipulated and changed include gridlines, arrows, legend (key), axis, data chart markers and data marker patterns. These are reviewed in later units.

At the end of this unit you will be able to

■ select a chart type, such as bar, area or column

■ select a chart format, such as the type of bar or pie chart

■ add attached and unattached text

■ select and edit or delete text

■ move unattached text

■ change text font, alignment and orientation.

What you need

To complete this unit you will need

■ the document file **Users** last used in Unit 16.

To date we have used the default chart format, which is the column chart. To explore other formats that are available, click on the down arrow of the

Chart Type button or use **Chart-Chart Type** and select a chart type.

Options include: bar, area, column, line, pie, combination, XY scatter, 3-D area, 3-D bar, 3-D column, 3-D pie and 3-D line. These are listed in the **Chart Type** dialog box. The **Custom types** tab offers some further options.

Note: It is important to choose chart type first as any subsequent formatting applies to a specific chart type.

Task 1: Using chart type

Using the last chart that you created experiment with displaying the data in different formats and chart types, by investigating the options under **Chart Type**. Note that some chart types are more suitable than others for your data. Good charts are charts that suit their purpose. To add data labels as illustrated, select **Chart-Options**, and click on the **Data Labels** tab. Select Show value.

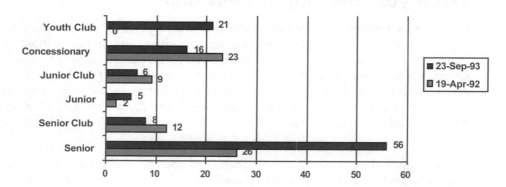

Hints for good charts

Since there is a wide range of different chart types available the most difficult decision is the choice of the correct chart type to effectively display a specific data series. To some extent this is a matter of personal preference, but the set of hints below offers some general guidelines that you may wish to consider. Some of these hints relate to points that you will master in Unit 18, but they are summarised here for completeness.

1   Think about the appearance of the chart when it is printed on paper. It is easy to get carried away when you are designing a chart on a coloured screen. Think about whether the data series that are shown will be sufficiently differentiated when printed on a non-colour printer. Test this.

2   Do not display too many data series on one chart; three is often sufficient.

3   When using bar or column charts distinguish between when composite and normal bar or column charts are appropriate. Think about which data you are comparing with which other data.

4   Use 3-D charts sparingly. Only simple 3-D charts look effective on paper.

5   Only use pie charts to display parts of a whole. It is inadvisable to explode more than one segment. The format which is often most helpful shows data labels and percentages.

6   Use line graphs to join distinct data points. Use different data markers to denote different data series.

7   Check that the chart has a title, axes labels, data and, when more than one data series is displayed, a legend.

8 Try not to cover data markers with text such as titles or the legend. If necessary move text and legend.

9 Examine the chart for legibility. Turn the tick mark labels round or change their size if necessary.

10 Remember that the most effective charts often show a very limited set of data, effectively labelled.

11 Only use gridlines sparingly.

12 When creating a number of charts in a document, try to develop a style so that comparable data appears on a similarly formatted chart.

Working with chart text

The following table summarises the key operations that you may wish to perform on chart text.

To	Do this
Add attached text	Choose **Chart-Chart Options-Titles**. Select the appropriate part of the chart to which you wish to add text. Type in text. Click on OK. The text appears in black selection squares. Press *Esc*.
Add unattached text	Type the text required. The text appears in black squares indicating that you can move and size the text. Press *Esc*. This text is in a text box.
Select text	Click on the text.
Edit text	Select text, then retype it, or position the insertion point within the text and insert or delete characters. Press *Esc*.
Delete text	Select text, and press the *Delete* key.
Move unattached text	Select text, to show the border surrounding the text, drag to the position that you want.
Display data labels, values or percentages	Switch to Chart window. Choose **Chart-Chart Options**, and select appropriate options. Click **OK**.

The chart text font, alignment and orientation can be changed. In addition it is possible to change the pattern and colour of the text area and the colour, weight and style of the border around the text. To illustrate this process we will consider changing the orientation of axis labels on the x-axis from horizontal to vertical.

■ Select the axis

■ The name of the selected component will appear in the box on the toolbar.

■ The text can be formatted using either the buttons on the toolbar or using **Format-Font**, or **Format-Selected Axis**.

■ Experiment with setting different fonts and text alignments, using both toolbar buttons and the wider range of options offered through the dialog boxes.

Task 2: Adding labels and headings

It is time that we added some axis labels and a title to our chart and investigated any other formatting that might be necessary. In the document **Users** double click on the chart that compares Junior data with Junior Club Data. We will add some labels to this, so that it starts to look like the chart below.

1 Once you are in Graph click on the chart to select it.

2 Choose **Chart-Chart Options**. Type the title (e.g. Attendance Figures) in the Chart title box. Choose **OK** . This appears in black selection squares. To remove these squares, press *Esc*.

3 Choose **Chart-Chart Options**. Type in the text e.g. Week Commencing, in the **Category (X) axis** box. This appears in black selection squares. To remove these squares, press *Esc*.

4 Choose **Chart-Chart Options**. Type in the text e.g. Number, in the **Value (Z) axis** box. Press *Esc* to remove the selection squares.

5 You will observe that adding labels tends to shrink the size of the chart display. Stretch the chart to a suitable size, taking care not to exceed the margins.

6 The chart as shown below also features some additional formatting as described in Unit 18.

7 Insert the chart into the document **Users**, and save the document.

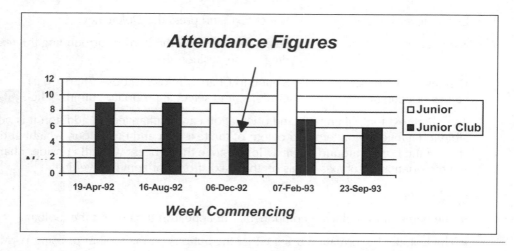

More chart formatting

What you will learn in this unit

This unit focuses on additional chart formatting, such as formatting axes, gridlines, legends and data labels. At the end of this unit you will be able to

- format axes
- format gridlines
- add, place and format the legend or key
- insert data labels.

Every feature of a chart can be modified or formatted in the same way. Many of the options to perform these operations are under the **Chart Options** menu. First, however, before you can format or edit a chart item, it must be selected.

When a chart item is selected it is marked with either white squares or black squares and a border, depending upon its type. Chart items and text marked with white squares or handles and a border can be formatted with commands and moved or sized with the mouse. Chart items and text marked with only selection squares cannot be moved or sized directly. Some items, such as axis labels, can be formatted or realigned with commands. It is useful to review the means for selecting parts of charts.

To	Do this
Select an item	Click on the item
Select a series	Click any marker in the series
Select a single data marker	To format a single data marker, click it once to select the series, again to select the individual marker, and then double-click it to display the Format Data Point dialog box
Select gridlines	Click on a gridline
Select axis	Click the area containing the axis tick mark labels
Select the entire plot area	Click any area in the plot area not occupied by another item
Select the entire chart	Click anywhere outside the plot area, where there is not another item

The table below summarises some of the key operations necessary in order to format axes, gridlines, legends and data labels.

To	Do this

Legends

Add a legend	Choose **Chart-Chart Options-Legend-Show Legend**
Delete a legend	Choose **Edit-Clear** or set via **Show Legend** as above.
Move a legend	Drag it to a new position
Format the border and the legend box	Choose **Format-Selected Legend**. Under the area of **Patterns** tab select the border and area options that you want. To format the legend text font, choose the **Font** tab, and select the options that you want

Gridlines

Format gridlines	Select one of the major gridlines for the axis, and choose **Format-Selected Gridlines**. Select the style, colour and weight, and choose **OK**

Axes

Show axes labels	Click on **Chart-Chart Options-Axes**, and select to display appropriate axes
Format the axes scale	Click on axis to be formatted. Choose **Format-Selected axis** and choose the **Scale** tab. Enter the appropriate values or select or clear boxes to achieve the scale format required
Format axes patterns and tick mark label location	Select an axis to be formatted. Choose **Format-Selected axis** and choose the **Patterns** tab. This will cause the **Patterns** dialog box to be displayed. Under **Axis** select type, style, colour and weight for the axis line. Select the major and minor tick mark types. Under tick mark labels, select the position on the chart where the tick labels are to appear. To format the tick mark label font choose the **Font** tab. To format the orientation of the tick mark labels, choose the **Alignment** tab and select the options that you want. Choose **OK**

Data labels

Show data labels	Choose **Chart-Chart Options-Data Labels** and select appropriate labels
Format data labels	Select data labels to be formatted. Choose **Format-Format Data Labels**. Select the options that you wish to apply to your chart, and choose **OK**
Clear the data labels format	Select the marker, and choose **Edit-Clear**. Select the **Clear** option

Task 1: Exploring further formatting

The objective of this task is to encourage you to explore some of the formatting features of Graph. There is not space here to deal with these in detail, but here are a few things that have been used on the chart above and which you might like to try.

1   Select the chart that you were working with in Unit 17, Task 2.

2   Select the title by clicking on it (the border with black selection squares is displayed). Choose Format-Selected Chart Title and choose Font then change the format of the text to, say, italic and a larger font size.

3   Select each of the axis labels in turn. Choose Format-Selected... and change the format of the text using the Font tab.

4   Select each of the axes in turn. Choose Format-Selected Axis and choose Patterns. In the dialog box, change the tick mark type for major to cross and for minor to none.

5   Move the legend by first clicking on it to select it and then dragging it to a better position.

6   Exit Graph, and in Word display the drawing toolbar, using View-Toolbars-Drawing. Click on the arrow and insert an arrow onto the graph.

7   Examine your chart in the document and save the document again as Users.

Editing a chart

The Edit menu can be used for manipulating charts as for pieces of text. First click on the chart to select it, then you can copy or clear a chart or undo changes to a chart as described below.

Copying a chart

To copy a chart choose Edit-Copy. Graph copies the chart to the clipboard. Switch to the application where you want to position the chart. Choose Edit-Paste. Note that the new copy, while still selected, floats, and can be moved by using the arrow keys.

Clearing a chart

To clear a chart select the entire chart in the Chart window. Choose Edit-Clear. Choose All, Formats or Contents depending upon whether you wish to clear both data and formats or only formats or only data.

Undoing changes

To reverse changes use Edit-Undo.

Note: There are no direct tasks attached to this activity, but you should find these operations useful in managing the charts in the other tasks.

Task 2: Creating a new chart and using it in a document

Traffic Consultants Fogg and Co are concerned for the local residents in the vicinity of Kibbleworth, and have commissioned a study of the number of commercial and private vehicles travelling along the main access road. Create a chart displaying the following data and insert the chart in a document.

	Sun	Mon	Tues	Wed	Thurs	Fri	Sat
Private	33	34	51	47	63	19	39
Commercial	1	26	25	20	37	15	12

1 First create a column chart showing both data series. Do not forget to add axes labels and a title.

2 Format the title and the axes labels appropriately.

3 Format any other features of the chart that you would like to change, such as the axes.

4 Insert the chart into your document.

5 Make a further copy of the chart and use the datasheet associated with this copy to create two more charts.

6 Select each data series in turn, i.e. Private and then Commercial, and display each of these on separate bar charts, both of which you should insert into your document.

7 Choose appropriate formatting and check that the axes labels and title are appropriate.

Task 3: Creating a pie chart

Use a pie chart to display the following data concerning the use of a health and fitness centre in 1995.

Step Aerobics	Popmobility	Aerobics	Keep Fit
5058	4779	2080	679

Remember to add a title and experiment with the use of data labels, possibly as percentages. Save this chart in a document called **Aerobics**.

Images in documents

What you will learn in this unit

Word allows a graphic image to be created and inserted into a document. Graphic images are integral parts of many documents and the drawing toolbar offers a means to construct them from within the word processor.

In this unit the basic features of the drawing toolbar are explored. At the end of this unit you should be able to create

■ basic shapes from which images can be created

■ simple images and diagrams.

Drawings are invaluable in many documents, for example in presenting plans or layouts. Box and line diagrams are widely used in many scientific and technical documents.

In Word there are two types of image, those that 'float' over the text and those that do not, known as in-line images. Images that 'float' over text are not displayed in normal view; they are only displayed in page layout view. In-line images can be seen in both normal and page layout view. Floating images are more flexible in the ways in which they can be positioned on the page but can be a little tricky to work with. They are the default type of image.

Displaying the drawing toolbar

The Drawing toolbar can be displayed by clicking on the **Drawing** button in the standard toolbar. The drawing toolbar is displayed at the bottom of the screen. Clicking on the **Drawing** button in the standard toolbar will toggle the display of the drawing toolbar. The drop-down lists and buttons on the toolbar are the drawing tools and functions.

Drawings can be created either directly in page layout view or they can be created as a picture. In page layout view you may draw directly on the text on your document. The drawing can remain fixed at that position on the page or it can be anchored to a paragraph so that it will move with the text. This sort of drawing is a floating image which is only visible in page layout view.

A drawing may be created as a picture and for diagrams in a document this is the best method as the picture is a separate entity. The picture can be left as a floating image or changed into an in-line image which is also visible in normal view. To create a picture choose **Insert-Object** and choose **Microsoft Word Picture** and a drawing workspace will be displayed.

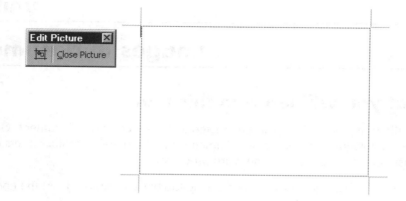

You can create your picture within the boundary shown, or if your drawing element is outside the boundary click on the **Reset Picture Boundary** button in the **Edit Picture** box to enclose all drawing elements in the picture boundary. When the picture is complete click on the **Close Picture** button to return to your document.

To edit a picture in a document simply double-click on it to display it in the drawing workspace.

Creating basic shapes

To draw lines click on the line drawing icon, position the pointer at the start of the line, click and drag to the end of the line. Lines may be freely positioned or they may start and end on invisible grid points. The following task investigates how the **Snap to Grid** feature on the drawing toolbar can be used to control this.

Task 1: Drawing lines

Start a new document and click on the **Drawing** button to display the Drawing toolbar. Choose **Insert-Object** and select **Microsoft Word Picture** to display the drawing workspace. Note that all the tasks will create drawings as separate entities but if you wish you may draw directly on your document in page layout view.

1   Click on the line drawing tool. In the drawing area the pointer changes to a +.

2   Position the pointer near the top of the area enclosed by the drawing boundary, click and drag towards the bottom of the drawing area. Don't release the mouse button just yet; notice how the line follows your pointer movements in a rather jerky fashion.

3   Release the mouse button and a line is drawn.

4   Click on the **Draw ▼** button on the drawing toolbar and choose **Grid**. This displays the **Snap to Grid** dialog box.

▦ Grid...

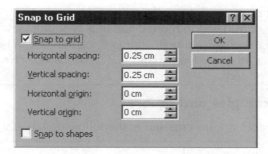

Notice that the **Snap to grid** check box is checked. This is the reason for the jerkiness of the line positioning. When **Snap to grid** is checked lines start and finish on invisible grid points. This is useful for maintaining consistency in a drawing. Through the **Snap to grid** dialog box the spacing of the invisible grid can be customised.

5   Remove the ✓ in the **Snap to grid** check box and repeat the line drawing exercise. This time notice that the end of the line should follow your pointer movements smoothly.

6   Experiment with drawing lines of different thickness and style.

Different line styles may be selected by clicking on the **Line Style** button in the toolbar. A menu of styles appears which can be selected from or the **Format AutoShape** dialog box can be displayed by clicking on **More** .

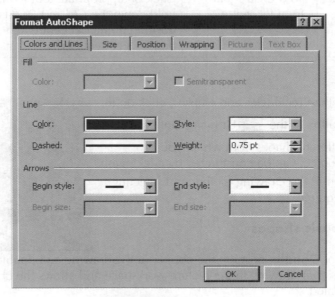

7   Click on the **Close Picture** button to return to the document. Select the picture and choose **Format-Picture**. Select the **Position** tab and remove the tick

from the Float over text check box, which turns the picture into an in-line image. Floating images will be considered in more detail in a later unit. Save the document as **Doodle**. Once a drawing is embedded in a document it can be manipulated in the same way as an embedded chart, i.e. its size can be changed and it may be cut, copied and pasted.

Drawing ellipses, circles, rectangles and squares

The methods for drawing these shapes are summarised in the following table.

Ellipse/circle	Rectangle/square	
To draw an ellipse from the corner of an imaginary bounding box	To draw a rectangle from one corner	Click on appropriate tool icon, position pointer at corner and drag to size required
To draw an ellipse from its centre	To draw a rectangle from its centre	Click on appropriate tool icon, hold down the *Ctrl* key, position pointer at centre and drag to size required
To draw a circle from the corner of an imaginary bounding box	To draw a square from one corner	Click on appropriate tool icon, hold down the *Shift* key, position pointer at centre and drag to size required
To draw a circle from its centre	To draw a square from its centre	Click on appropriate tool icon, hold down the *Ctrl* and *Shift* keys, position pointer at centre and drag to size required

Autoshapes

To draw shapes other than rectangles and ellipses, click on the **Autoshapes ▼** button in the Drawing toolbar. This displays a menu of different shapes from which you can choose. A shadowed object can be constructed by clicking on the **Shadow** button in the Drawing toolbar and selecting the type of shadow required.

Task 2: Creating basic shapes

1   Open the document **Doodle**, position the pointer in the drawing and double click. This displays your drawing in the picture workspace and allows the chosen drawing to be updated.

2   Create each of the shapes described in the preceding table. Experiment with the AutoShapes and shadows. Explore the effect that **snap to grid** has on the way in which the shapes are created.

3   Some of your shapes may go outside the drawing boundary. If so, click on the **Reset Picture Boundary** button. Save this drawing by clicking on **Close Picture** and using **File-Save** for revision in later tasks.

Note: To draw a rectangle or ellipse several times, double click on the tool you require. When you finish, click anywhere in the document to deselect the drawing tool.

Drawing arcs

By clicking on the arc drawing autoshape the pointer can be used to draw 90° segments (quadrants) of ellipses or circles.
Once the arc has been drawn it can be stretched or shrunk by dragging either end.

Task 3: Drawing arcs

For this task open the drawing from the document **Doodle** and add an arc to it.

1   Select the arc drawing tool from the AutoShapes. Position the pointer at one end of where the arc is to begin.

2   Drag to complete the arc. The direction in which the dragging is done determines which quadrant of an ellipse is drawn. If an arc of a circle is required hold down the *Shift* key during the dragging operation.

3   Click on the arc to select it and drag to change the angle of the arc.

4   Close the picture and save the document **Doodle**.

Drawing freeform shapes

Shapes composed of straight lines and/or freehand lines can be drawn using the Freeform button available in the Lines group of AutoShapes. A freeform shape may be closed, i.e. the beginning and the end of the shape join up, or it may be open. A closed shape can be filled with a colour and/or pattern.

Drawing a shape composed of straight lines

Click on the Freeform tool, position the pointer at the start of the shape, click, move the pointer to the end of the first line, click and repeat for each line in the shape. If the shape is closed, a polygon, when drawing the last line, to finish click near the beginning of the first line.

To create an open shape, when it is finished either press *Enter* or *Esc* or double click.

Drawing a freehand shape

Click on the Freeform tool, position the pointer at the start of the shape, click and drag to draw the shape. Do not worry if your drawing is shaky or inaccurate, Word offers the facility to edit the drawing, as described in the next unit.

An open or closed shape may be created as for a shape composed of straight lines.

Drawing a shape with both freehand and straight line sections

It is possible to alternate between drawing a straight line or drawing freehand to produce a composite shape. Use the move and click technique for drawing straight lines and a click and drag technique for the freehand sections. Open or closed shapes may be created.

Task 4: Creating an image

In a new picture to be created underneath the previous one in the document **Doodle** the techniques just described will be experimented with. The aim is to reproduce the image shown below. This image is composed of an AutoShape, the star, a closed shape, the 'leaves' of the tree, and one open shape, the tree trunk.

1   Position the insertion point below the previous picture in **Doodle** and choose **Insert-Object**. Select **Microsoft Word Picture** to start a new picture.

2   Click on the **AutoShapes** button and choose the five-point star tool from the Stars and Banners group. Click and drag a star in the picture workspace.

3   Click on the **AutoShapes** button and choose the Freeform tool from the Lines group. Draw the 'leaves' shape by positioning the pointer at the start of the shape

and clicking and dragging to draw the shape.

4   Finish the shape at the original start position so that a closed shape is formed.

5   To create the tree trunk start at the leaves, work down to the base and then back up. Experiment with combining freehand and straight lines to create this shape.

6   As this is an open shape, end the shape by double clicking.

7   Close the picture and save the document **Doodle**. Preview and print it.

Editing images, importing pictures

What you will learn in this unit

This unit continues from the previous one by examining ways in which images may be edited. At the end of the unit you should be able to

- edit previously created images
- add text to images
- import pictures produced by other applications.

Word can import pictures from a variety of sources, so whether you wish to incorporate some clipart or a scanned image into your document the process is simple. A company logo or a cartoon, for example, can easily be incorporated into a document.

Editing an image

It is very unlikely that a drawing will be right first time and parts of it will need to be altered or removed. An image is usually made of several parts, a different drawing tool may have been used to create each part, or there may be several parts created by the same tool. Each part of the drawing is known as an object. Each object may be selected and altered individually or objects may be selected together.

Selecting objects: arrow tool

The object which needs to be altered or deleted needs to be selected before changes can be made. Click on the **Select Objects** button on the **Drawing** toolbar to change the pointer to an arrow for selecting the required object.

Use the arrow to point to the object that is to be altered. If the object is filled then you may point to anywhere within the bounds of the object; if it is not filled then point to the outside edge of the object. The pointer changes shape to a four-headed arrow.

If the object is a line, clicking will cause a handle (small white box) to appear at each end. For other objects eight handles will appear. These handles are at the corners and the middle of the sides of an invisible rectangle surrounding the object.

The handles are known as resizing handles and can be used to edit the object.

Selecting more than one object

If the same editing action is to be performed on more than one object of the image, then more than one object can be selected. First consider where an imaginary box that would enclose all of the objects required would be. Using the arrow, point to one corner of this imaginary box and click and drag. A dotted line box appears. Make sure you have surrounded all the objects you wish to select, with this box, before releasing the mouse button.

An alternative method is to select each object in turn while holding down the *Shift* key.

Removing parts of an image

Select the part (or parts) of the image to be removed or cleared. By using **Edit-Clear** or using the *Delete* key the selected object(s) will be removed. Don't forget that you can use **Edit-Undo** if this goes wrong!

Moving and copying

Any object or group of objects can be moved from one location to another in a drawing. To move a single object, first select it and by dragging the four-headed arrow pointer the object can be moved to its new position. A ghost (a dotted outline of the object) will move across the screen as you move the mouse. Release the mouse button to drop the object in its new place.

To move a group of objects, first select the objects required. Click on any one of the objects in the group and then drag as for a single object.

Any object or group of objects can be copied using the normal Copy and Paste operation. First select the object or objects to be copied, use **Edit-Copy** and follow with **Edit-Paste**. A copy will be pasted into the drawing and can be moved to the appropriate place.

Task 1: Copy and paste

Double click on the drawing created in Task 4 of unit 19.

1　Select the star by clicking anywhere on its edge.

2　Using **Edit-Copy** and **Edit-Paste** make a copy of the star.

3　Move the copy by dragging it to another position in the image as illustrated below.

4　Close the picture and save the document.

Resizing an object

To resize an object the resizing handles, which appear when the object is selected, are used. Any one of the handles may be dragged to resize the object, bearing in mind that the object will behave as if it is pinned to the drawing with the opposite corner from the one that is being dragged.

The point at which the object is pinned is known as the anchor point. As an alternative to one of the corners of the bounding box being the anchor point, a central anchor point can be chosen. To do this hold down the *Ctrl* key during the resizing operation.

During resizing the object is displayed in the same way as during moving, that is, as a *ghost*.

Controlling height, width or proportions during resizing

To resize an object so that its proportion of height to width remains the same, hold down the *Shift* key while dragging a resize handle diagonally.

To resize an object so that its height or width remains unchanged, drag one of the central side handles.

Grouping objects for editing

You may wish to create a composite object which is composed of simpler shapes and then be able to work with the object as one for sizing and moving. Objects may be grouped which reduces the clutter of many sizing handles and also can speed operation as Word works faster with objects that are grouped. To group a set of selected objects click on the **Draw** button and select **Group** 🖽 G̲roup from the menu. When you have finished the editing then the objects may be ungrouped using the **Ungroup** option in the **Draw** menu. 🔲 Ungroup

Task 2: Resizing

Open the image from the previous task. Select one of the stars. By dragging one of the sizing handles make it larger, as illustrated below.

Editing freeform images

All freeform images are composed of lines connected end to end. Even freehand curves are made up of lots of little lines connected end to end. The point at which one line joins to the next is known as a **vertex**.

Before any changes can be made to a freeform it is necessary to display it in editing mode. Select the freeform and choose **Edit points** 🔲 Edit Points from the **Draw** menu. The freeform is shown with the vertices marked with little control handles. To see these more clearly it may be necessary to zoom in on your drawing (see below 'Moving around a drawing: zoom').

By dragging the control handles it is possible to edit the freeform. It may be necessary to check that the Snap to grid option is not checked; also it may be useful to zoom in on the drawing (see below). If there are a lot of vertices, some can be deleted. To delete a vertex, position the pointer on the control handle belonging to that vertex, hold down the *Ctrl* key and click. A line will join the remaining vertices either side of the one deleted. To add a vertex, point to the line where a vertex is to be added, hold down the *Ctrl* key and click.

Task 3: Editing a freeform

Open the image from the previous task.

1 Select the 'leaves' part of the tree.

2 Zoom in to part of it and choose **Edit points** from the **Draw** menu to display the control handles.

3 Drag the control handles to produce more detail in the shape of the freeform object.

4 Close the drawing and save the document.

Rotating or flipping an object

Rotating causes an object to be rotated either through 90° or any angle using the free rotate facility and flipping causes an object to become its mirror image. Rotating or flipping can be performed on one object or a group of objects. It does not work on text objects or bitmaps. Bitmaps are explained later in this unit.

↻	Free Rotate
↺	Rotate Left
↻	Rotate Right
⟂	Flip Horizontal
◁	Flip Vertical

Select the object or objects to be rotated or flipped and choose **Rotate or Flip** from the **Draw** menu. If rotating choose either **Free Rotate**, **Rotate Left** or **Rotate Right** from the menu; if flipping choose either **Flip Horizontal** or **Flip Vertical**. Notice that there is also a **Free Rotate** button in the **Drawing** toolbar.

Task 4: Rotate and flip

1 Recall the previous image and rotate left the star on the left of the drawing and flip vertically the star on the right of the drawing.

2 Select the right-hand star and choose Free Rotate, you will notice the object is bounded by an imaginary square with a small green circle at each corner.

3 Drag one of the circles to freely rotate the object.

4 Return to the document and save.

Lines and fills; colour and patterns

Objects such as rectangles, ellipses or other shapes can be drawn with or without lines (outside edges) and fills. It is possible to set no fill and no line for an object and it then becomes invisible, so take care when choosing settings. When first drawn an object has a line or fill defined by the settings of the **Autoshape defaults**. Changes to the defaults can be made by first creating an object with the desired characteristics and choosing **Draw-Set Autoshape Defaults**. The new setting affects only objects drawn after changes are made.

An object can have different settings from the drawing defaults by double clicking on the object or choosing **Format-Autoshape** and altering the settings in the **Format-Autoshape** dialog box.

Choosing lines and fills

The style and width of an object's outside line reflect the default settings under the **Colours and Lines** tab of the **Format-Autoshape** dialog box. Line style can be set using the **Line Style** and the **Dash Style** buttons on the Drawing toolbar or by choosing **Format-Autoshape**.

An object may be filled. Select the object and click on the **Fill Colour** button in the Drawing toolbar. Select a colour from the colour grid.

Instead of solid colour fills, shading and patterns may be used. Double click on the object and choose from the options in the *Fill* section of the **Colours and Lines** tab of the **Format-Autoshape** dialog box. Objects may be filled with solid colour, graded colour, patterns, textures and pictures.

Task 5: Filling

1   Continuing with the previous drawing, double click on the 'leaves' object.

2   Choose the **Colors and Lines** tab, open the **Colors** drop-down list and select
    green.

3   Choose a pattern by opening the **Colors** drop-down list and choosing **Fill Effect**.
    Select the **Patterns** tab and choose an appropriate pattern. Click on **OK** and
    OK again. You may wish to experiment with different fills and effects.

Overlapping objects

If an image is created where one object overlaps another then the most recently
drawn object will obscure the earlier object. Word treats the objects as if they are
stacked one on top of another, with most recent on top. This stacking order can be
changed by selecting an object and choosing **Draw-Order-Bring to Front** to put the
object on top of the stack or **Draw-Order-Bring to Back** to send the object to the
bottom of the stack.

Task 6: Overlapping

Add a moon selected from the AutoShapes basic shapes menu. With the 'moon'
selected choose **Draw-Order-Bring to Back**.

Moving around a drawing: zoom

Choose the level of magnification from the **Zoom** drop-down list box in the main toolbar. There are seven levels of magnification: 10%, 25%, 50%, 75%, 100%, 150%, 200% and 500%, and also Page Width, Whole Page and Two Pages. If 25% is chosen the image shown is reduced to a quarter of full size; if 200% is chosen the image is shown twice full size. Use the scrollbars to display the required portion of the picture on the screen.

Images and text

The full range of text fonts available to you within Word is also available to a drawing. Headings and labels can easily be part of the drawing. To put text into an image click on the **Text Box** button in the drawing toolbar and click on the picture to create a text box into which you can insert text.

Inside the text box will be an insertion point, which is where your text will appear as it is keyed in. When the text is complete simply move on to the next action you wish to perform. While the text box is still selected you can perform text formatting using the main tool and ribbon bar as usual. For example, the font, size, colour and alignment of the text can be adjusted. The text box itself can have its edge defined in the same manner as other objects.

Editing text

To add or correct text within the text box click on the text to place an insertion point in the text, so that additions and corrections can be made.

Task 7: Adding text

Add text to the drawing as shown.

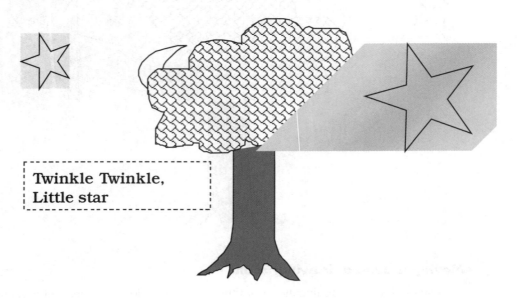

Importing pictures

As well as the clipart files supplied with Word, files containing pictures can be created by other applications. A picture file can be imported directly into a document using **Insert-Picture** or can be imported into a picture workspace in the same way. Two common types of picture file that are created by other Windows applications are formatted as either a bitmap or a Windows metafile. Other formats as well as these may be imported, for example, .gif and .jpg formats used for pictures in Web pages.

A bitmap stores the image as being made up of many tiny squares known as pixels. Other formats store the image as being made up of objects such as lines, ellipses and rectangles, Word is able to 'decode' this information, so enabling more flexibility for editing the imported image.

To insert a clipart picture use **Insert-Picture Clip Art** and the **Microsoft Clip Gallery** dialog box appears.

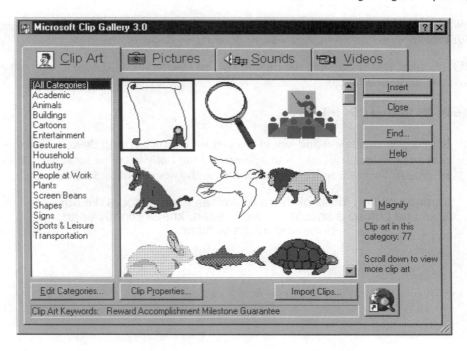

Select the category you require, scroll through the clipart images until you find a suitable image, select it and click on **Insert**. Note that clip art images are inserted as floating images but you may convert them to in-line images.

To insert a picture from file use **Insert-Picture From File** and the **Insert Picture** dialog box appears.

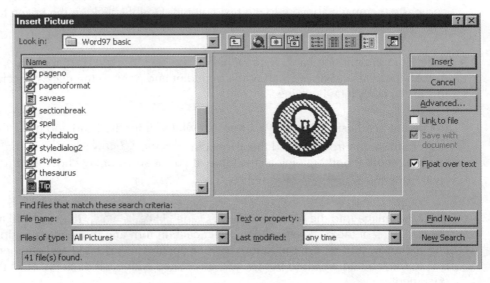

In the **Look in:** box, select the folder (directory) in which the picture file is situated. From the **Name** box select the file required. All picture files that Word recognises will be listed in the Name box. After selecting the file click on Insert and the file will be imported into the document or drawing workspace.

If Float over text is checked the picture will be inserted as a floating image, otherwise as an in-line image.

Task 8: Images in tables

1   Start a new document and key in the text for the picture and then display the drawing toolbar. The head is an ellipse and the body is constructed from a series of straight lines. Close the picture and save the document as **Stickman**.

Starting position for all of these exercises is on all fours. Hands should be placed a shoulder's width apart, knees slightly apart, arms and thighs vertical.

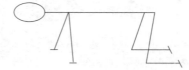

2   Start a new document while **Stickman** is open. Select and copy the picture above and paste it into the new document. Save this document as **Stick** for use later. Close **Stick** so that **Stickman** becomes the current document.

3   In the next part of the task two images are created side by side by putting them into a table. Set up a table that is two columns wide and one row deep. Copy and paste the image above into the first column. Double click on the image to edit it.

4   Delete the straight line back. Redraw half of the back using the arc tool (in AutoShapes, basic shapes). Start at the midpoint and draw to the neck. Stretch this arc to complete the spine.

5   Rotate the head using free rotate. Choose a white fill for the head and bring the nearer arm to the front. To add the arrow click on the Arrow button in the Drawing toolbar and drawing a small line. If you wish you may chose an arrow style using the Style Arrow button.

6   Copy the image into the second column. Using Flip Vertical , flip the head and the two parts of the back separately. Select each in turn and move into position. Flip the arrow and reposition. Return to your document, save and add another row to the table in which to put the text associated with each diagram. Save the document.

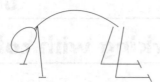 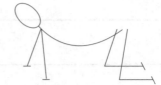

Arch the back, at the same time look down at the floor.

Lower the stomach towards the floor, at the same time look up towards the ceiling.

Task 9: A logo

1 Start a new document and switch to page layout view. If necessary, click on the drawing button in the main toolbar to display the Drawing toolbar.

2 Click on the button and draw a text box. Choose a thick line for the edge of the box. Add the text, choosing appropriate font, alignment and paragraph spacing.

3 Click on the ellipse tool and add a circle. Save the document.

Recreate the same logo using the drawing workspace (**Insert-Object-Microsoft Word Picture**). Investigate the difference between the way Word displays the two logos in Normal and Page Layout views.

Working with columns

What you will learn in this unit

This unit is the first of two that help you to integrate skills that you will have developed by following the tasks earlier in this series, and introduces the use of columns and associated document formatting that might help you to produce a document such as a newsletter. At the end of this unit you will be able to

■ create a document that uses columns.

Earlier units offered an opportunity to create a long and integrated document. This set of units is also integrative, but focuses on the creation of relatively short documents such as newsletters that integrate text, formatted in various ways, with graphics and images. In the design of such documents there is a significant emphasis on the page layout, so it is useful to work in Page Layout view, and to remember to make full use of Print Preview before printing the document.

The newsletter that we wish to create is printed at the end of the text for this unit. Note that it is designed to occupy two pages in this text, and is not exactly two pages of A4 in length, since the page size is shorter than A4. Note that the newsletter includes text, text in tables, graphics and an image. There is scope for additional formatting. Here we introduce the basics. You may develop these by, for instance, applying more ambitious border design or shading. The newsletter that you will create in this unit is not a real newsletter. It has been designed to allow you to experiment with the use of a range of formatting facilities within columns.

Word is primarily suitable for the design of simply formatted newsletters. It does, however, offer a wide range of desktop publishing features, and you will need to evaluate whether it is appropriate for any more significant applications that you might have, or whether to opt for a desktop publishing package.

Most of the skills that you will need in order to create this newsletter have already been introduced in earlier tasks. We will walk through these operations here for consolidation, and to develop confidence with their use in conjunction with one another. You should be reasonably confident with these earlier tasks, because it is not possible to cover everything that you might do wrong in this session! First, however, you will explore the new concept of columns.

 You may find that in these units more than in any of the earlier units you have applied some formatting and are unable to retrieve the situation. Do not forget to make use of **Edit-Undo**.

Working with columns

Word allows you to produce two types of columns. You have already met the columns in tables, which are parallel columns. The second kind of column is the snaking column, in which text flows from the bottom of one column to the top of the next, as in newspaper columns.

Document views

When entering text you will probably have used Normal view most of the time. This is easy for fast text entry, but does not display columns side by side.

Page Layout is preferable when using columns, as it shows columns side by side with items such as graphics in the correct location. It is useful for editing, manually inserting column breaks, and adjusting column width. You can zoom in or out.

Print Preview shows the overall page layout, just as the document will be printed. You can edit text, and make adjustments to margins and page breaks.

Creating multiple column layout

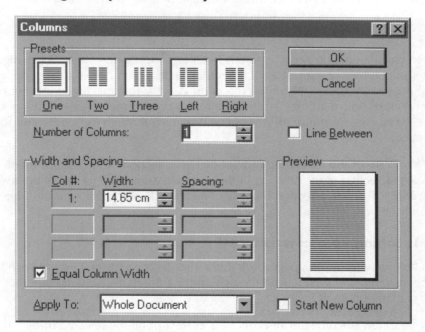

To create a multiple column layout

1 choose **View-Page Layout**

2 click in the section to be formatted

3 use **Format-Columns**

4 specify the number of columns, for example, 2

5 In the **Apply To:** box, select the portion of the document that you want to format

6 Choose **OK** .

Alternatively

1   choose **View-Page Layout**

2   click in the section to be formatted

3   click on the **Columns** button on the toolbar

4   drag to the right to select the number of columns that you want.

When you release the mouse button, Word formats the section that contains the insertion point.

You can also use the **Columns** command to:

- change the space between columns, through the **Width and spacing** section

- add a vertical line between columns, through the **Line between** box

- format the current section to start in a new column through the **Start New Column** box.

You can change the number of columns in all or part of a document. To change the number of columns on part of a document, make that part a separate section by inserting a section break. Within each section Word automatically adjusts the width of the columns. Word adjusts the space between columns to create equal amounts of space. You can customise this for unequal spacing through the **Width and spacing** section.

Note: Word stores the formatting instructions for a section in the section mark. If you delete a section mark, any text in the section assumes the format of the text below it. If you delete a section break accidentally, do not forget your old friend **Edit-Undo**.

Task 1: Setting up a newsletter

In this task we wish to set up the basic format for the newsletter. First we wish to add the heading, and then to insert the columns, and finally, we will enter the address at the bottom of page 2.

First open a new document. Check that the correct printer is selected using **File-Print**. Also choose the correct page size using **File-Page Setup**. Choose **View-Page Layout**, then type Chelmer Leisure and Recreation Centre, *Enter*, Fitness News across the top of the document. Press *Enter* to make some space in the document below the text. Next format this heading, as described below.

1   Apply centre justification.

2   Select a type font and face that cause the first line to fill the width of the page.

3   Format the text to bold.

4 Create some space above and beneath the text (Hint: use spacing before for the first line of the title and spacing after for the second line).

5 Place a border around the heading by selecting it then using the **Border** button.

6 Next we wish to create two columns.

7 Place the insertion point below the heading.

8 Choose **Format-Columns**.

9 Select the number of columns below the heading, i.e. **2**.

10 Select This point forward in the **Apply To:** box.

11 Check the **Line Between** check box.

12 Choose **OK**. Word places a section break between the heading and the multiple columns.

13 Finally save this document, using **File-Save**, as **News1**.

Task 2: Putting text into columns

With the document **News1** open, start to enter the following text at the top of the first column. Format the heading appropriately. Notice that the text is formatted into the first column.

The Benefits of Exercise

Whallop! It's hit you!! When your most energetic event over the last few weeks was getting up to change the TV channel because the remote control wasn't working, you suddenly realise that physical exertion can be quite unpleasant!

But fear not! After only a short spell at an activity class the benefits will start to show. You can expect an increase in stamina (those stairs won't seem so steep anymore), strengthening and toning of your once invisible muscles, and an increase in the range of movement of those aching joints.

Save the document as **News1**.

Charts and images in multi-column documents

What you will learn in this unit

At the end of this unit you will be able to

- insert a chart or image in a multi-column document
- size an image or a chart
- use indents in columns
- use tabs in columns
- use tables in columns.

Charts and images can be imported into multi-column documents in much the same way as they are imported into a single-column document. The main differences are

- they may be too big to place in one column and may therefore need sizing or need to occupy two columns
- we may wish to display them across more than one column.

What you need

To complete this unit you will need

- the image from document file **Stick** created in Unit 20
- the document file **News1** created in Unit 21
- the chart saved in the document **Aerobics** created in Unit 18
- the document **Times** created in unit 8.

Sizing an image or chart

To size an image or chart

- select the chart or image
- drag a sizing handle on the graphic until it is the size that you want.

For more precision you can measure the width of each column and add to that the space between the columns. Select the graphic and use Format-Picture to make the total measurement equal to the width of the graphic. You may also need to adjust the height of the graphic.

Task 1: Importing an image into the newsletter

We wish to import the image created earlier called **Stick**, into our document **News1**.

1 Place the insertion point below the existing text.

2 Open the image file **Stick**. Click on the image and use **Edit-Copy**.

3 Move back to the window showing **News1** and apply **Edit-Paste** to insert the image into the document.

4 If necessary, size the image by clicking on it to select it and dragging its handles to fit the column. Add a thin line border.

Task 2: Adding a bordered advert to the newsletter

Next, at the bottom of the first column we would like to insert the following advertisement.

> **New Fitness Centre**
>
> **Fight the Flab**
> in Chelmer Leisure and Recreation Centre's
> New Fitness Suite
>
> *Opening 12th September 199X*

1 Move the insertion point below the image and type in the advertisement to fill the first column.

2 Centre all of the text and format it appropriately.

3 Apply a border by first selecting the text, and then selecting from the Borders toolbar or using **Format-Borders and Shading**.

Working with hanging indents, tab stops and tables in columns

Hanging indents, tab stops and tables can be used in columns in much the same way as they are used in single column documents. The only problem is likely to be that if you have originally created a table in a single-column format and then try to insert it into a two-column document, for instance, it will probably be too wide and will need reformatting.

157

Task 3: Using indents

In this task you will insert the following text into the second column of **News1**, using a hanging indent.

1 At the top of the second column on the first page enter ***Summer 199X***. In order to get to the top of the second column use **Insert-Break** and choose **Column break** to force a column break.

2 Centre this text, format it and place a border around it. To make a new line press *Enter* but this carries forward the formatting from the previous line. To remove this it is easiest to reapply the Normal style. Open the **Style** box and select Normal.

3 Type in the heading for the list shown below and centre it.

4 Press *Enter* to move onto the next line.

5 Click on the numbering icon for automatic numbering. Use **Format-Bullets and Numbering** to alter the font of the numbers using **Customize and Font**.

6 Type in the text below.

Six Sun Safe Tips For Sensible Tanning

1. Apply sun cream 30 minutes before going out in the sun and use sun cream all year round.

2. Avoid sun bathing between 11.00am and 3.00pm.

3. Reapply sun cream regularly - cream can be removed by swimming, sweating and drying off.

4. Pace yourself! - don't take too much sun too soon. Melanomas take a few days to develop.

5. Keep babies and small children out of strong sun.

6. Always use moisturiser after sun bathing to prevent dry skin and peeling.

---

7 Place a border around the text using **Format-Borders and Shading**.

8 Add the paragraph of text shown at the bottom of the second column of the newsletter.

9 Save the document as **News1**.

Task 4: Using tabs

In this task we insert part of a document that uses tabs into our column.

1   Insert a column break to place the insertion point at the top of the first column on the second page.

2   Open the document called **Times**, and select the part of the document relating to the Health and Fitness Suite opening times.

3   **Edit-Copy** this selection.

4   Return to the Window displaying the newsletter, and choose **Edit-Paste**.

5   You may need to move the tab stops in order to align the text appropriately. Select the text and experiment with different tab stop positions by dragging them on the ruler, and if necessary use different font sizes. You may wish to abbreviate the text slightly. Try to fill the column.

Task 5: Using tables

In this task we introduce a table into a column.

1   Insert the text shown at the bottom of the first and top of the second column on the second page in the newsletter, entitled 'Fat, where's it at?'.

2   Choose **Table-Insert Table**. Choose three columns.

3   Enter the text shown in the table on the newsletter into the table, using *Tab* to move between cells.

4   Apply a border to the table using **Format-Borders and Shading**. Choose an appropriate line.

Task 6: Inserting a graph

In this task we add a graph to the newsletter we created in the last unit.

1   First type in the text entitled 'Step Aerobics'.

2   Now, open the document **Aerobics** created earlier, or quickly create this document. **Aerobics** contains a small pie chart.

3   Select the pie chart and use **Edit-Copy**.

4   Return to the Window that displays the newsletter and use **Edit-Paste**. The chart should appear in the newsletter.

5 You may wish to size the chart to make it fit the column, by clicking on it to select it and then pulling its handles.

6 Save the document as **News1**.

Now perform the formatting for the bottom of page 2.

7 Choose **View-Header and Footer**.

8 Switch to the footer and type in the following text.

For bookings and details of any activities and classes at Chelmer Leisure and Recreation Centre Please Ring: 091-336-6612.

9 Format the text to a size that makes it legible

10 Place a border around the text, using **Format-Borders and Shading**.

11 Click on the **Close** button.

Task 7: Creating a simple leaflet

This task asks you to create the text that follows the newsletter as one side of a leaflet or flyer.

The text uses three columns and some text formatting. This task should be much simpler than the one that you may just have completed on the newsletter. Here are the basic steps.

1 Open a new document.

2 Choose **File-Page Setup** and alter the page orientation to landscape.

3 Choose **Format-Columns** and select three columns to *apply* to the *whole document*.

4 Enter the text in the first column. Apply borders, centring and character formatting as appropriate.

5 Continue to type in the text for the next two columns, formatting it as appropriate.

Chelmer Leisure and Recreation Centre

Fitness and Health Suites

Fully air conditioned

Satellite TV

Computerised video screen

Cardio-vascular equipment

Fitness testing

Super circuit training

Sauna and steam rooms

Jacuzzi relaxation lounge

Sunbeds

Personalised diets

Beauty therapy

A unique combination of superb facilities

The Health and Fitness Suites represent a superb facility.

Fitness Suite

The fitness suite is for all sizes, ages and fitness levels. It offers an environment where care and attention to users' needs are of paramount importance.

Each person is carefully assessed and taught how to use the equipment to maximise their potential. Don't worry about your level of fitness - our staff are on hand to help and advise you on how to progress enjoyably and safely.

Super Circuit Training. For the energetic, special Super Circuit training sessions are available.

Personalised Exercise Programmes and Fitness Testing Option. Personalised exercise programmes are available with an added option of a fitness test.

Fitness testing has become an important ingredient in the recipe for improved fitness. It tells you your current fitness level and provides a tailor made programme with personal fitness targets.

Health Suite

Our superb health suite offers all of the facilities necessary to relax, unwind and let the day's worries drift away. These include:

Sauna & Steam Room. Relax in either the Sauna or Steam Room. Ideal after a hard workout, long day or simply for pure relaxation.

Power Shower. Whether you like your showers hot or cold foam, spray or jet, we have just the shower to suit your needs.

Jacuzzi Relaxation Lounge with Satellite TV. Immerse yourself in jets of warm water and gently soothing bubbles while you unwind and alleviate stress from work and everyday life.

Sunbeds. Our three new Ultrabronze tanning beds use the latest RUVA tubes and also offer high pressure facial panels.

Task 8: Creating a page containing single and multiple columns

This task asks you to create a front page which uses columns for part of the page.

1   Open the document **Front** that you created earlier.

2   Choose View-Page Layout.

3   Remove all borders.

4   Place the insertion point below the centred text.

5   We wish to reposition the student's and tutor's name to display it as indicated below. Select the text at the bottom of the page.

6   Choose Format-Columns, select two columns and apply to selected text.

7   Place the pointer at the end of the tutor's name and insert a column break with Insert-Break-Column Break and then OK .

8   Now select the text in the first column and apply left alignment.

the Manchester Metropolitan University

Crewe + Alsager Faculty

Environment & Enterprise Project

The Refurbishment of the Multi-Gym into a Fitness Suite

at Chelmer Leisure and Recreation Centre

A Feasibility Study

By: Sarah Leveridge   *Course: HND Business and Finance*

Tutor: R. S. Symmond   *Date: 1st February 1995*

Chelmer Leisure and Recreation Centre
Fitness News

The Benefits of Exercise

Whallop! It's hit you!! When your most energetic event over the last few weeks was getting up to change the TV channel because the remote control wasn't working, you suddenly realise that physical exertion can be quite unpleasant!

But fear not! After only a short spell at an activity class the benefits will start to show. You can expect an increase in stamina (those stairs won't seem so steep anymore), strengthening and toning of your once invisible muscles, and an increase in the range of movement of those aching joints.

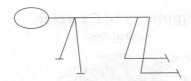

New Fitness Centre

Fight the Flab

in Chelmer Leisure and Recreation Centre's
New Fitness Suite

Opening 12th September 199X

Summer 199X

Six Sun Safe Tips For Sensible Tanning

1. Apply sun cream 30 minutes before going out in the sun and use sun cream all year round.

2. Avoid sun bathing between 11.00am and 3.00pm.

3. Reapply sun cream regularly - cream can be removed by swimming, sweating and drying off.

4. Pace yourself! - don't take too much sun too soon. Melanomas take a few days to develop.

5. Keep babies and small children out of strong sun.

6. Always use moisturiser after sun bathing to prevent dry skin and peeling.

The month is May, the sun may shine and the melanomas may not be too far behind. The need for creaming up has never been greater!

The strength of your cream is governed by its SPF - Sun Protection Factor. This gives you an indication as to how long you can stay in the sun without melting. The higher the SPF the greater the protection provided. The choice of an appropriate SPF depends upon your skin type and how it usually reacts to the sun.

Opening Times

Health Suite

Monday	9.00am - 9.00pm	Ladies Only
Tuesday	9.00am - 9.00pm	Mixed
Wednesday	9.30am - 9.00pm	Mixed
Thursday	9.00am - 1.00pm	Ladies Only
	1.00pm - 9.00pm	Mixed
Friday	9.00am - 9.00pm	Men Only
Saturday	9.00am - 1.00pm	Men Only
	1.00pm - 5.00pm	Mixed
Sunday	9.00am - 5.00pm	Mixed

Fitness Suite

Monday	8.00am - 8.00pm	
	8.00pm - 9.00pm	Super Circuit
Tuesday	9.00am - 9.00pm	
Wednesday	9.30am - 8.00pm	
	8.00am - 9.00pm	Super Circuit
Thursday	9.00am - 9.00pm	
Friday	9.00am - 9.00pm	
Saturday	9.00am - 5.00pm	
Sunday	9.00am - 5.00pm	

Fat, where's it at?

Fat plays an important part in all our lives. It is widely accepted that reducing fat from our diet is a positive move but does that mean all fat?

Saturated fats, the most unhealthy, are fats which are solid at room temperature. Examples include animal fats and brazil nuts. Mono-unsaturated fats can either be solid or liquid at room temperature and these include vegetable fats and olive oil. Fats which are soft or liquid at room temperature are polyunsaturated. These can be found in fish oils and vegetable oils.

A fatty diet can result in obesity with many of its attendant health risks: high blood pressure, diabetes, gall bladder disease, arthritis, surgical risks and coronary heart disease, to name but a few. The table below shows the recommended limits on fats for the average *quite active* person.

	Saturated Fat	Other Fats
80Kg Man	35g	82g
61Kg Woman	27g	63g

Step Aerobics

The chart below shows how popular Step Aerobics has become. Have you tried step aerobics? It is a popular means of getting and keeping fit.

Popularity of Exercise Classes

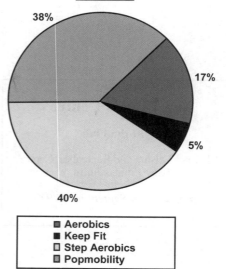

- ■ Aerobics
- ■ Keep Fit
- □ Step Aerobics
- ▨ Popmobility

For bookings and details of any activities and classes at Chelmer Leisure and Recreation Centre please ring:

0191-336 6612

Floating images and text boxes

What you will learn in this unit

In Units 19 and 20 we have considered in-line graphics, i.e. those that do not float over the text. However, the effects 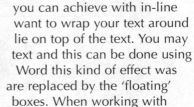 you can achieve with in-line graphics are limited and you may want to wrap your text around a graphic or allow the graphic to lie on top of the text. You may want to have different areas of text and this can be done using text boxes. In earlier versions of Word this kind of effect was achieved by using frames, which are replaced by the 'floating' properties of graphics and text boxes. When working with floating images you need to be in Page Layout view.

For floating images, you have a choice of several specific positions or a measured fixed position. You can position objects at the top, centre or bottom of a page, and at the left, centre or right of a page. You can also designate an exact location by specifying measurements.

You can choose how you want text outside the floating image to wrap around it.

Text boxes allow text to be rotated and flipped, and colour, fill, shadow, 3-D effects etc. can be incorporated. You can also control the width of a paragraph inside a text box frame so that its lines are a specific length.

It is easy to move the floating images and text boxes, and see their relation to other elements on the page, but you must remember to work in Page Layout view. At the end of this unit you will be able to:

■ draw images onto the text

■ add a clipart image as a floating image

■ move, size and delete floating images

■ control text wrap

■ add a text box

■ add special effects to text boxes

■ position an image or text box.

What you need

To complete this unit you will need

■ the document file **Openday** created in Unit 4.

Creating a floating image

Working in Page Layout view you may draw directly on a document using the drawing tools discussed in earlier units. By setting the text wrap options you can control the way in which your image is displayed. If clipart is added as a floating image then it may be treated in the same way.

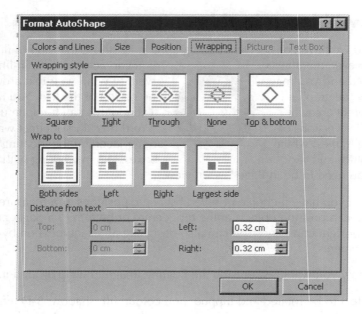

Task 1: Drawing floating images onto the text

1 Key into a new document the first two paragraphs of the text used in Task 6 of Unit 5, or open this document if you saved it.

2 Create a stylised drawing of a mouse, as illustrated below, by first drawing an ellipse onto the text. Set the text wrapping to Tight using the **Format AutoShape** dialog box. If the text does not wrap check that you do not have 'Keep lines together' formatting on the paragraph.

This example, and the one at the top of the unit, are really bad examples of the use of tight text wrapping because the surrounding text is difficult to read. More appropriately tight text wrapping should be used where the graphic is at the edge of the text or spans two columns.

3 Complete the drawing using simple shapes, filling in the eyes and nose with black. The tail was created using the curve tool found in the Lines category of AutoShapes.

The mouse is a hand-held device connected to a computer that can be used as an alternative to the keyboard for issuing commands or instructions. Its shape resembles a mouse with a ⬡⬡ cable for a tail and buttons for eyes. Unlike a real mouse the cable emerges from between the eyes! The operator's hand grips the mouse between thumb and little finger allowing the first and second fingers to rest over the buttons.

Sliding the mouse over the desk top, ideally using a mouse mat, beside the computer, rotates a direction sensitive ball inside which in turn causes a pointer to move around the screen.

4   Group all the shapes by selecting them, choose the **Select Objects** pointer from the **Drawing** toolbar and use it to draw a rectangle around the image.

5   Choose **Draw-Group** to group the objects, which can then be moved and sized. Don't forget to deselect the **Select Objects** pointer by clicking on its button on the Drawing toolbar before proceeding to your next action.

Image control: moving, sizing, deleting and copying

To move an image point to it. The pointer should change to a four-headed arrow. Click and drag the image to a new position. When dragging you will see a dotted *ghost* indicating the position of the image as it follows your mouse movements. Releasing the mouse button will drop the image in its new position. Clicking on the object to select it will display the sizing handles that can be dragged to change the image's size.

With the image selected, if the *Delete* key is pressed the object will be deleted.

Objects may be cut or copied and pasted, as illustrated in the following task.

Task 2: Adding clipart

In this task, clipart will be added to a document as a floating image.

1   Open the document **Openday** in Page Layout view.

2   Use **Insert-Picture-Clip Art** and add the tick clipart from the Shapes category. Set the text wrapping to square and resize the image to make it smaller.

3   Move the image to the right-hand side of the 'Step' paragraph. Copy and paste the image twice so that there is a tick image for each paragraph. Experiment with arranging these images on the right-hand side and then the left-hand side of the page. You may also position them in either the left or right margin.

4   Save the document.

Controlling text wrapping around a graphic

In the previous two tasks you have met tight and square text wrapping. There are also through, none, and top and bottom wrapping. As well as selecting wrapping style you can select which side or sides of the image to wrap to. The 'Distance from text' section allows the amount of space between the object and the text to be controlled.

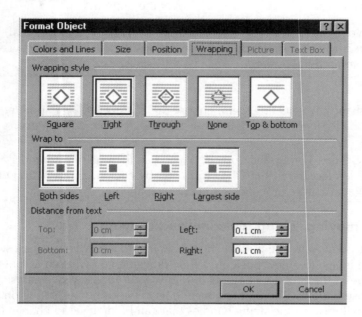

Task 3: Investigating text wrapping

Recall the document created in Task 1 and investigate various settings of text wrapping and distance between text and object.

Text boxes

A text box is an area that you can create in a document in which text can be positioned in the same way as a graphic. This can give effects such as a portion of text in a box straddling two columns, the text in the text box often being an interesting snippet of the main text, usually in a larger type, thereby drawing your attention and inviting you to read it.

Text in text boxes may be orientated either horizontally or vertically, creating another way in which interest can be added. A long, thin, vertically orientated text box at the edge of a page could be used effectively in a flyer.

Text boxes may be linked, i.e. text in one box may 'flow' into text in another and so on. All of the effects that you can create with text boxes are from the realms of publishing, rather than word processing, so you would do well to study newspapers, newsletters, magazines, adverts etc. that you come across in your daily life to give you ideas for text layout.

Layout is important. Typographers and graphic designers study for years to learn how to achieve the right balance on a page. So, initially you may find it easier to copy the layout of something you see that looks good rather than trying to design your own layout. Once you have done this a few times you can have fun trying out different layouts, and incorporating both graphics and text boxes in your documents.

To create a text box

1 With your document in Page Layout view click on the **Text box** button in the **Drawing** toolbar and draw a rectangle on your document.

2 Your insertion point is inside a bordered text box ready for you to enter text.

3 You may draw as many text boxes as you like onto your document.

To allow text to flow from one box to another

1 Click on **View-Toolbars-Text Box** to make the Text Box toolbar appear.

2 Click in the first text box then click on the **Create text box link** button in the Text Box toolbar and click in the second text box.

3 If you have more than two text boxes that you wish to link you may link the second to the third by clicking in the second text box then clicking on the **Create text box link** button in the Text Box toolbar and clicking in the third text box. This can be repeated to link third to fourth text boxes etc.

4 To remove a link, use the **Break forward link** button in the Text Box toolbar.

5 To move between linked text boxes use the **Previous text box** and **Next text box** buttons on the Text Box toolbar.

To change text orientation

1 Click on the **Change text direction** button.

Task 4: Adding text boxes

In this task a text box straddling columns will be created.

1 Make a copy of the leaflet created in Unit 22. Change its orientation to portrait and reduce the number of columns to two.

2 Click on the text box tool and draw a text box in the upper central part of the document so that it straddles the two columns.

3 Select the text A unique combination of superb facilities and cut it and paste it into the text box.

4 You may wish to adjust fonts and position the text box in a similar way to that illustrated.

Task 5: Text box special effects

In this task text orientation and text box shadowing will be investigated. This task and the previous one should give you a basis from which to experiment with text boxes in your own documents.

1 Make another copy of the leaflet created in Unit 22. Change its orientation to portrait but leave the number of columns as three.

2 Adjust the widths of the columns using **Format-Columns**, remove the tick from the equal width check box and make the first column 2cm wide. Leave the other columns as the width that Word adjusts them to.

3 Draw a text box in the first column large enough to fill it. Cut and paste the heading Chelmer Leisure and Recreation Centre into the text box.

4 Change the orientation of the text to vertical and adjust its size and character spacing.

5 Select the text box and add a shadow effect.

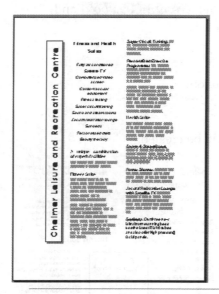

Positioning an image or text box

You can position an image or text box relative to an element on a page, for example, a margin.

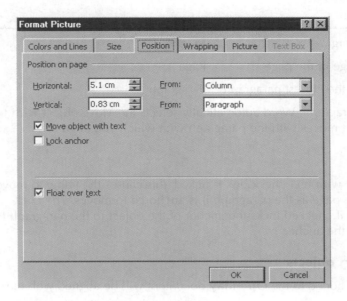

To position an image horizontally

1 choose **View-Page Layout** to view the document in Page Layout view. Click on the image or text box to select it

2 choose **Format-Picture** (**Object** or **Text box**). In the **Position** tab, under **Horizontal:** type a fixed position for the object (distance from the left edge of the item shown in the **From:** box)

3 in the **From:** box, select one of the following as the measuring point for the horizontal position.

To align the object	Select
Relative to the left margin	Margin
Relative to the left edge of the page	Page
Relative to the left edge of the column	Column

4 choose the **OK** button.

To position an object vertically

1 view the document in page layout view, and select the object you want to position

2 choose **Format-Picture** (**Object** or **Text box**). In the **Position** tab, under **Vertical:** type a fixed position for the object (distance from the top edge of the item shown in the **From:** box)

3 in the **From:** box, select one of the following to set the measuring point for the vertical position.

To align the object	Select
Relative to the top margin	Margin
Relative to the top edge of the page	Page
Relative to the top of the closest paragraph	Paragraph

Note: If you select Paragraph, Word automatically selects the **Move object with text** check box. The object moves with the paragraph with which you align it.

4 Click on **OK** .

5 If the **Move object with text** check box is ticked, this causes the frame to move up or down on the page as the paragraph it is anchored to moves. The **Lock anchor** check box if checked locks the anchor of the object to the paragraph that currently contains the anchor.

Task 6: Positioning objects

In this task the clipart added to the **Openday** document will be aligned with the margin.

1 View **Openday** in Page Layout view. Select one of the clipart pictures by click-ing on it.

2 Choose **Format-Picture** and choose the **Position** tab. Note the settings for hori-zontal and vertical.

3 In the horizontal section alter the distance and click on **OK** . Note the effect. Repeat the formatting, investigating the effect of choosing Margin, Page or Column in the **From:** list box.

4 Experiment with choosing different formatting for vertical positioning of a clipart picture.

Setting up a drop capital letter

When you are creating chapter titles or section headings in a book or brochure, you may want to create an initial capital letter that is larger than the remaining text in the title. This is called a drop capital letter, because you can vary its alignment on the line.

The top of the drop capital usually aligns with the top of the first line of text, but you can adjust this by adding space before the text. You can also adjust the blank space between the drop capital letter and the text.

To set up a drop capital letter

1   change to Page Layout view

2   click the paragraph that you want to begin with an initial, or dropped, capital letter. The paragraph must contain text

3   choose **Format-Drop Cap**

4   click Dropped or In Margin. Use None to remove a dropped capital

5   select any other options you want and click on   **OK** .

Task 7: Drop capital letter

Open the document **Promote**. The aim of this task is to add a drop capital to the beginning of each paragraph.

1   Use **View-Page Layout** to view **Promote** in Page Layout view. Save the document as **Dropcap**.

2   Set the font formatting of this document to Times New Roman, size 12. Using paragraph formatting, set the spacing before all of the paragraphs to 6pts.

3   Click in the first paragraph and choose **Format-Drop Cap**. Select **Dropped** and click on   **OK** .

4   Click in the second paragraph and choose **Format-Drop Cap**. Select **In Margin** and click on   **OK** .

5   Save the document as **Dropcap**.

Symbols, calculations and multi-level bullets

What you will learn in this unit

This unit concentrates on specialised symbols, which can be used for

- foreign words

- simple mathematical and scientific formulae.

Other slightly more advanced techniques that can be used in document creation will be examined in this unit, these being

- performing calculations

- using fields

- interfacing with other software.

Scientific, mathematical and foreign symbols

For normal work the letters and symbols that appear on the keyboard are sufficient. However, there may be occasions where a foreign word containing symbols that are not in the English alphabet needs to be included. Another area in which non-standard letters are required is in the production of a scientific or mathematical document.

For mathematical use, the Windows Symbol font contains the Greek alphabet and a variety of mathematical symbols. In the font Normal Text there are foreign characters.

To insert a symbol or foreign letter

1   position the insertion point where the character is to appear

2   use Insert-Symbol. The Symbol dialog box appears. Select the Symbols tab

3   open the drop-down Font: list box, select the particular font required and all the symbols available in that font will be displayed in a matrix. For foreign text choose (normal text), for mathematical symbols choose Symbol and for fun characters choose Wingdings

4   a symbol is selected using the pointer by pointing and clicking. The chosen symbol is displayed in a larger size as white text on a blue background (default colours)

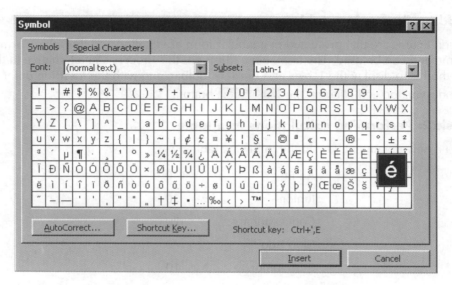

5   to insert the symbol into the document click on **Insert** . The symbol will take the current point size that is being used. Close the **Symbol** dialog box by clicking on the **Close** button if you have inserted a symbol or **Cancel** if you have not.

Task 1: Using scientific, mathematical and foreign symbols

Start a new document, and, selecting symbols from (normal text) and Symbol, key in the following.

Fête   café Σx $a \geq b$ 100°C

Defining foreign language portions of a document

If a portion of a document, or indeed all of it, is to be written in a foreign language then Word needs to be made aware of this. You will not want Word to spell check a paragraph in, say, French using an English dictionary. If French proofing tools (spelling and grammar) are available these are used instead.

To format text as being in a foreign language

1   select the text

2   choose **Tools-Language-Set Language** and in the dialog box select the language required. Click on **OK** .

Calculations

Basic mathematical calculations can be performed within a Word document. Word allows figures to be added, subtracted, multiplied and divided. Word assumes that you will perform calculations in a table, in a manner similar to using a spreadsheet. It also offers some spreadsheet formatting and functions, such as MAX, MIN, and AVERAGE. The **Formula** command which is available on the **Table** menu is the method Word uses to perform calculations.

Adding figures in a table

Often figures are that presented in a tabular form are totalled and the **Table-Formula** command can be used. The task below illustrates this process. An alternative to this method is to display the **Tables and Borders** toolbar, and with the insertion point in the destination cell click on the **AutoSum** button.

Task 2: Performing calculations in a table

Into a new document, key in the following table.

Adult	140
Junior	20
Concessionary	70
Club Adult	20
Club Junior	10
Total	

1   Position the insertion point in the cell in the table where the answer is to appear, i.e. the empty cell opposite Total.

2   Choose **Table-Formula**. A **Formula** dialog box appears in which Word proposes a formula, in this case =SUM(ABOVE), which means it will total the column above the cell selected. Click on **OK** and the answer, 260, will be inserted into the table.

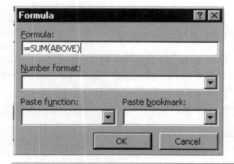

Task 3: Simple formulas

Start a new document. Enter the following table with which some simple formulas will be used.

3	4	
3	4	

1   Position the insertion point in the empty cell at the top of the third column.

2   Choose **Table-Formula**. A **Formula** dialog box appears in which the proposed formula is =SUM(LEFT), which means it will total the row to the left of the cell selected. Click on **OK** and the answer, 7, will be inserted into the table.

3   Imagine that each column in the table is denoted by a letter of the alphabet (so in the table above there are columns A, B, and C) and that each row in the table is denoted by a number (rows 1, 2, and 3). Each cell in the table can be uniquely identified by its 'grid reference', i.e. the top left cell is A1 and the bottom right cell is C3. If you have used a spreadsheet you will be familiar with this concept.

4   Position the insertion point in cell C2. Use **Table-Formula** and edit the proposed formula so that it reads =A2*B2 instead. Click on **OK**. The * means multiply. Is the answer what you expected?

5   Position the insertion point in cell A3. Use **Table-Formula** and edit the proposed formula so that it reads =C2/A1 instead. Click on **OK**. The / means divide.

6   Position the insertion point in cell B3. Use **Table-Formula** and edit the proposed formula so that it reads =C2-C1 instead. Click on **OK**. The - means subtract.

7   Position the insertion point in cell C3. Use **Table-Formula** and edit the proposed formula so that it reads =SUM(A1:C2) instead. Click on **OK**. What has been calculated? Keep this document open while you read the next paragraph.

Using fields

Fields are instructions to Word to perform a certain task. You will probably have inserted fields into a document without realising it. With the document from the last task still open choose **Tools-Options**, select the **View** tab and under **Show** check the **Field codes** tick box. You should see the numbers change into their underlying formulas, enclosed in curly brackets. These are codes, which are instructions to Word to perform the calculation. Use **Tools-Options** again to change back to the usual view by removing the ✓ from the **Field codes** check box.

Fields can be quite complicated and it is not the intention to go into very much detail on this subject. Therefore only two types of fields which might be used in the type of work produced by a reader will be considered. These are the date field and sequence numbering fields. Having a flavour of these may encourage the more serious user to experiment with other field types.

Task 4: Using a date field

A date field is particularly useful in a standard letter or memo template. This exercise will insert an updateable date field into the file **Appmemo**. Open the file **Appmemo** created in Task 3 of Unit 3.

1   Position the insertion point at the place where the date is to go.

2   Choose **Insert-Date and Time**.

3   Select the format of the date from the **Date and Time** box.

4   Check the **Update automatically** box. This will insert the date as a field. Click on **OK**.

The date field will not automatically update so that if you were to open the memo in a few days time the date would still be that of when the field was created. To update the field

5   Select the date.

6   Press *F9*.

Using fields to sequence numbers

This field type is useful if you have a numbering sequence for chapters, sections, paragraphs, figures, tables etc. in your document. It saves having to check back through the document to see what the last number in the sequence was. To insert a sequence field

1   position the insertion point at the place in the document where the number is to go.

Either

2   choose **Insert-Field**, then select **Numbering** from **Categories:** and **Seq** from **Field names:**.

3   Click in the **Field codes:** box after **Seq** and type the name of the sequence of numbers, e.g. table for a sequence of numbers for tables. Click **OK**.

Or

2   Press *Ctrl+F9* and inside the curly brackets (which are not ordinary curly brackets) type seq table.

3   Press *F9*.

This kind of field code may be viewed individually by positioning the insertion point in the field, clicking the right mouse button and selecting **Toggle Field Codes**. This shortcut menu also offers an alternative way of updating the field by choosing **Update Field**.

Note that care must be taken to ensure that the fields are updated. For example, a table might be added or removed from the document. Fields may be updated individually as described for the date field or in the case of a sequence the whole document can be selected and all fields will be updated by pressing *F9*.

Task 5: Sequencing fields

For this task create a document containing some tables from Unit 9.

1 Open a new document.

2 Using **Insert-File** insert the following documents into the new document: **Times**, **Fatlim**, **Address** and **Timetable**.

3 Leave a line space between each table.

4 Below each table

 ■ type Table

 ■ press *Ctrl+F9* and shaded curly brackets appear

 ■ in between the curly brackets type seq table

 ■ press *F9* to turn the field into a number.

5 Save the document as **Tables**.

Interfacing with other software

Word interfaces well with other Windows applications, particularly those written by Microsoft. It will also interface with other software.

Importing text files

It is possible to import text that has been directly created by another word processor or by previous versions of Word. When **File-Open** is used if **All Files** (*.*) is chosen from the **Files of Type:** list box then all files in the directory are listed. Many word processors produce documents files with the extension .doc but text files may have other extensions such as .txt or .rtf.

If a file is selected that was not created by Word, then Word will automatically convert it.

Exporting files for use with other software

To do this use **File-Save As** and open the **Save File as:** list box. Select the type of format required and save as normal. For example, the document can be saved in a WordPerfect for Windows format.

Interfacing with other Windows applications

Within windows the clipboard can be used to import text or graphics from other Windows applications. The ability to interface with Excel has already been mentioned. Graphics, for example, from the Windows Paint application, can be imported via the clipboard.

Multi-level bullets

As well as creating straightforward bulleted and numbered lists, Word also allows you to create lists within lists, known as multi-level lists. The following task illustrates the creation of a multi-level list.

Task 6: Multi-level lists

1   Type in the following list as a bulleted list without the indents.

2   Select the entire list and choose **Format-Bullets and Numbering**.

3   Click on the **Outline Numbered** tab and select the multi-level bullets. Click on **OK** .

4   Position the insertion point in the second point and click on the **Increase Indent** button on the formatting toolbar. Repeat for the other indented points.

> ❖   Fitness Suite
>
> ➢ Super Circuit Training
>
> ➢ Personalised Exercise Programmes
>
> ❖   Health Suite
>
> ➢ Sauna and Steam Room
>
> ➢ Power Shower
>
> ➢ Jacuzzi Relaxation Lounge
>
> ➢ Sunbeds

5   You can modify the bullets by selecting the whole text again and choosing **Format-Bullets and Numbering**. Choose **Customize** . In the **Level** box select level 2.

6   Open the **Number style:** list box. Scroll down to **New Bullet**. In the **Symbol** dialog box select a font and choose a symbol for the bullet. Click on **OK** .

7   Experiment with adding additional points and selecting their level using the **Increase/Decrease Indent** buttons.

8   Try using numbers and a combination of numbers and bullets in a multi-level list. You will find Word provides a selection of choices in the Outline Numbered gallery.

What you will learn in this unit

On completion of this unit you will be able to

- create a standard letter
- create a set of data
- perform a mail merge.

The word 'mailshot' is commonly used in the business environment. It means to send out many duplicated letters to a target audience, often for advertising or market research. A word processor's mail merge facility can 'personalise' a standard letter so that, for example, the recipient's name and address are printed. This unit explains how to use Word to perform a simple mail merge.

Two documents are required for a mail merge

- the **standard letter**. This contains the standard text plus areas that are marked as 'replaceable', i.e. personal information can be slotted into them
- the **data document**. This is a document containing the personal information that is to be slotted into the standard letter. Each person's information is in a separate paragraph.

First make a plan of the standard letter to decide which information is to be replaceable. In this example the replaceable information is name, company, street, town, county and postcode. If you browse forwards you will see the layout of the letter. It is simplest to create both of these documents in the same directory. Word will help you through three stages of mail merging.

Task 1: Mail merging

The first stage is to create the standard letter (the main document).

1   Open a new document.

2   Key in the address of the centre, using a date field for the current date, as follows.
Chelmer Leisure and Recreation Centre
Park View Road
Chelmer
Cheshire
CE9 5JS
12th October 199X

3　Save the document as **Mail**.

4　Choose Tools-Mail Merge and the Mail Merge Helper dialog box appears.

5　Click on the ▐ **Create** ▐ button. The active window, **Mail**, becomes the Choose **Form Letters** and click on basis for the form letters. the ▐ **Active Window** ▐ button. The next step is to specify the data source or to create the data source.

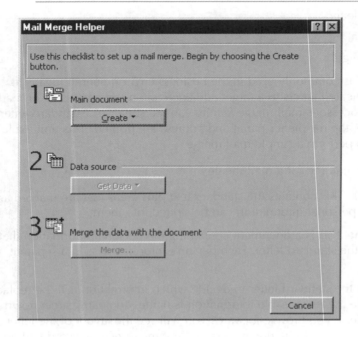

6　Click on the ▐ **Get Data** ▐ button. Choose Create Data Source and the Create Data Source dialog box is displayed. In this box you define the names of your replaceable fields.

7　Click on **FirstName** (in the Field names in header row: box) and click on the ▐ **Remove Field Name** ▐ button. Repeat for all fields except Title, LastName, Company and PostalCode.

8　Type Street into the Field name: box and click on ▐ **Add Field Name** ▐. Repeat for Town and again for County. Use the 'Move' arrow buttons to reorder the field headers so that they are in the order Title, LastName, Company, Street, Town, County and PostalCode.

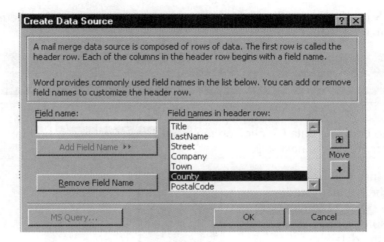

9   Click on   **OK** . Save your data source as **Supplier**.

10 Choose   **Edit Data Source**   and a form for entering data records will be displayed.

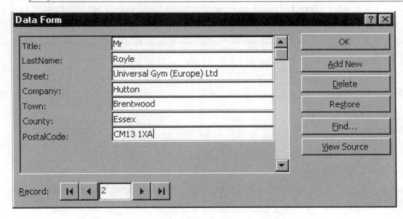

11 Enter the following records. Hint: use the Tab key to move from one box to the next. After each record is entered click on the   **Add New**   button, until the last one is complete, and then click on   **OK** .

Title	LastName	Company	Street	Town	County	PostalCode
Mrs	Allen	Medlock Leisure Centre	Fold Avenue	Droylsen	Tameside	DR17 5TG
Mr	Royle	Universal Gym (Europe) Ltd	Hutton	Brentwood	Essex	CM13 1XA
Mr	Bradbury	Atlanta Sports Industries Ltd	Atlanta House	Maltby	Rotherham	S66 8QN
Miss	Jackson	Physique Training Equipment Ltd	Bankfield Mill	Colne	Lancashire	BB8 9PD

12 Save this as **Supplier**. You will return to the letter document. Notice that there is an extra toolbar for mail merging.

13 If you wish to edit your data file click on the **Mail Merge Helper** button; otherwise carry on to the next step.

14 Position the insertion point for the first line of the company address. Click on the **Insert Merge Field** button to display a drop-down list of the fields in the data file.

15 Click on Company.

16 Press *Enter* for the next line of the address, click on the **Insert Merge Field** button and highlight **Street**. Build up the address and greeting as shown below. Remember to insert a space between the Title field and the LastName field.

<<Company>>

<<Street>>

<<Town>>

<<County>>

<<PostalCode>>

Dear <<Title>> <<LastName>>

Thank you for your interest in providing equipment for our new fitness suite. Please could you submit a formal quote for our consideration.

Yours sincerely

G. V. Richards

Manager

---

17 Save these additions to the document **Mail**.

18 You may wish to click on the **Check for Errors** button in the Mail Merge toolbar to check the data file. The most common error is where the number of fields in a record does not correspond with the number of fields that have been specified. Choose the option 'Simulate the merge and report errors in a new document'.

19 Click on the `Merge to Printer` button in the Mail Merge toolbar to print the merged letters. One letter will be produced for each record of data.

20 If you wish to merge the letters to a file rather than printing them, this can be done by clicking on the `Merge to New Document` button on the Mail Merge toolbar. Each letter in the new document will be separated from the next by a section break. Don't forget to save this new document if you wish to keep the merge for later printing.

Printing envelopes and labels

As well as producing the merged letters Word provides a facility to print envelopes or labels by merging an address list. These two facilities will be explored in the following tasks.

Task 2: Printing envelopes

1 With the standard letter created in the last task still open, choose **Tools-Mail Merge**.

2 Click on the `Create` button and choose Envelopes. Next choose `New Main Document`.

3 Click on the `Get Data` button. Next click on **Open Data Source**, and select the directory of the file **Supplier.doc**. Click on `Open` after highlighting this file. Next click on `Set Up Main Document`.

4 On the `Envelope Options` tab, select the envelope size you want, and adjust the address format and position on the envelope. On the `Printing Options` tab, make sure that the selected envelope feed options are correct for your printer, and then click `OK`.

5 In the **Envelope Address** dialog box, insert the merge fields for the address information as shown below.

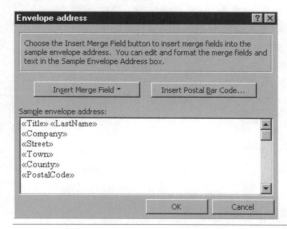

6   Click on **OK** and you will be returned to the Mail Merge Helper dialog box. Click on the **Merge** button.

7   In the Merge To box, choose New Document or Printer. If you choose Printer the envelopes will be printed straight away; choosing New Document will allow for later printing. Click on **Merge** .

Note: It is possible to print envelopes only for selected addressees by clicking Query Options, and then specify criteria for selecting the data records.

Task 3: Printing labels

The steps to printing labels are essentially the same as those for printing envelopes. In the second step choose Mailing labels and in step 4 select the type of labels you require.

Equation Editor

What you will learn in this unit

This unit introduces the equation editor and shows you how to

■ add complex formulas to your documents.

One of the most difficult tasks in word processing is to write an equation, particularly if the equation has a complicated structure. Lining up numerator and denominator, positioning brackets, using subscripts and superscripts, to name but a few, are typical of the problems encountered when constructing an equation. Word provides a means to overcome this in the form of an equation editor. The equation editor will not be examined in detail; however, the basics will be covered.

The Equation Editor works in the same way as Graph, i.e. the equation is constructed using Equation Editor toolbars and is then embedded into the document by clicking outside the equation. As with Graph, the equation may be edited by double clicking on it to return to the editor program.

Starting the Equation Editor

The Equation Editor is available through the **Insert-Object** command. From the object dialog box choose **Microsoft Equation 3.0.** Click on **OK** to select this option. Notice that other 'objects' can be activated through this dialog box. If this object is not available then you may need to install it. Close Word and any other applications and, using Office 97's add/remove components, add the Equation Editor which you will find in the Office Tools category.

The Equation Editor floating toolbars should appear and an equation editing work space. Note that only the menu bar and ruler remain at the top of the screen.

The Equation Editor toolbars

The Equation Editor toolbars are composed of two palettes, the symbol palettes and the template palettes. The insertion point looks different; it is flashing vertical and horizontal lines inside a dotted rectangle, in the equation editing work space, known as a slot.

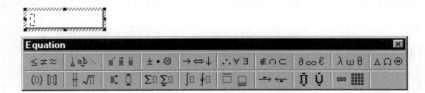

Building an equation

It is best to write down the equation to be created so that its method of construction can be considered. The basic rule for creating an equation is to set up a template first and then fill the slots in the template with symbols. If the wrong template is inserted by mistake use **Edit-Undo** to remove it.

Templates are chosen from the lower palette bar. The icons in this bar represent the categories of template. By clicking and holding the mouse button on one of these icons a sub-menu appears showing all the templates available in that category. Still holding the mouse button down, move to the one required and release the button. Symbols can be inserted into the template to complete the equation.

It is beyond the scope of this unit to go into very much detail concerning equation creation. However, by illustrating the creation of some basic statistical equations encountered by business students, it is hoped to provide a firm base from which to explore the capabilities of the Equation Editor.

Task 1: Creating an equation for the mean of grouped data

The equation to be produced is that for calculating the mean value of a set of grouped data.

$$\bar{x} = \frac{\sum fx_{mid}}{\sum f}$$

Start a new document.

1 Position the insertion point at the place where the equation is to be and use **Insert-Object-Microsoft Equation** 3.

2 Type x. Click on the third icon on the symbols bar. Click on the first box in the fourth row.

3 Type =. It is worth noting at this point that you cannot type a space into an equation; the editor sorts out the spacing.

4 Click on the second icon on the template bar. Click on the first box in the first row.

5 Click on the fourth icon on the template bar. Click on the first box in the first row.

6 Type fx.

7 Click on the third icon on the template bar. Click on the second box in the first row.

8 Type mid.

9 Click on the denominator part of the equation.

10 Using a template, insert a $\sum$ as for the numerator.

11 Type f. Click outside the working area to embed the equation in the document.

Task 2: Creating an equation for standard deviation

Keeping open the document just created, save it as **Stats**. On a new line create the following equation for the standard deviation of ungrouped data.

$$\sigma = \sqrt{\frac{\sum(x - \bar{x})^2}{n}}$$

1 Position the insertion point at the place where the equation is to be and use **Insert-Object-Microsoft Equation** 3.

2 Click on the ninth icon on the symbols bar. Click on the letter that is first on the sixth row. Type =.

3 Click on the second icon on the template bar. Click on the first box in the fourth row.

4 Click on the second icon on the template bar. Click on the first box in the first row.

5 Click on the fourth icon on the template bar. Click on the first box in the first row.

6 Click on the first icon on the template bar. Click on the first box in the first row.

7 Type x-x.

8 Click on the third icon on the symbols bar. Click on the first box in the fourth row.

9 Press ➡ to move the insertion point to the end of the brackets.

10 Click on the third icon on the template bar. Click on the first box in the first row. Type 2.

11 Click on the denominator slot. Make sure the insertion point is flashing in this slot.

12 Type n. Click outside the working area to embed the equation in the document.

Task 3: Creating the equation for the gradient of a line of best fit

Finally, add the equation to find the gradient of a line of best fit.

$$m = \frac{\sum xy - \frac{\sum x \sum y}{n}}{\sum x^2 - \frac{\left(\sum x\right)^2}{n}}$$

1   Position the insertion point at the place where the equation is to be and use **Insert-Object-Microsoft Equation 3**.

2   Type m=. Click on the second icon on the template bar. Click on the first box in the first row.

3   Click on the fourth icon on the template bar. Click on the first box in the first row. Type xy-.

4   Click on the second icon on the template bar. Click on the first box in the first row.

5   Click on the fourth icon on the template bar. Click on the first box in the first row. Type x.

6   Click on the fourth icon on the template bar. Click on the first box in the first row. Type y.

7   Click in the denominator slot of this part and type n.

8   Click in the main denominator slot to move the insertion point into it.

9   Click on the fourth icon on the template bar. Click on the first box in the first row. Type x.

10 Click on the third icon on the template bar. Click on the first box in the first row. Type 2.

11 Press ⬇ and type -.

12 Click on the second icon on the template bar. Click on the first box in the first row.

13 Click on the first icon on the template bar. Click on the first box in the first row.

14 Click on the fourth icon on the template bar. Click on the first box in the first row. Type x and press ➡ twice to move the insertion point to the end of the brackets.

15 Click on the third icon on the template bar. Click on the first box in the first row. Type 2.

16 Click in the denominator slot.

17 Type n. Embed the equation in the document. Save.

Adjusting settings in the Equation Editor

To make adjustments to the font and size of an equation use either **Style-Define** or **Size-Define**. **Style-Define** will allow different fonts to be applied and **Size-Define** will allow the size of the individual parts that make up an equation to be altered.

AutoFormat

What you will learn in this unit

When you are creating a document the best way to achieve a professional effect is to use styles. Styles enable you to be consistent throughout the document, for example, in your use of headings. If you are fairly new to using Word then applying styles may seem a little difficult. To help overcome this difficulty Word has an autoformatting facility which will apply an attractive format to your text by applying a built-in style.

As you add text to the document then AutoFormat can be applied to this to maintain the consistency of your document. If you have already applied some formatting to the document the AutoFormat facility can uniformly apply this to the rest of the document. At the end of this unit you will be able to

- choose AutoFormat options

- AutoFormat simple documents

- review AutoFormatting changes.

Setting up AutoFormat

Before using AutoFormat you should review the AutoFormat settings. There are two categories, AutoFormat and AutoFormat As You Type. To display the AutoFormat settings use **Tools-AutoCorrect** and click on the **AutoFormat** tab.

This dialog box allows you to set rules that Word's autoformatting facility will follow.

Apply

Headings	Automatically applies Heading 1 through Heading 9 styles to headings; for example, the headings in outlines or legal documents
Lists	Automatically applies list and bullet styles to numbered, bulleted and multi-level lists. Word removes any manually inserted numbers or bullets before automatically applying the built-in list or bullet styles
Automatic bulleted lists	Automatically adds bullets to a list
Other paragraphs	Automatically applies paragraph styles other than the styles for headings and lists, such as the Body Text style

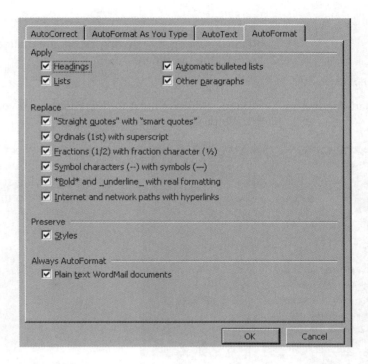

Replace

Straight quotes with smart quotes	Changes straight quotation marks (" and ') to "smart" (curly) quotation marks ("" and '')
Ordinals (1st) with superscript	Automatically changes normal typing into superscript where it is being used for an ordinal e.g. 9th
Fractions with fraction character	Converts ordinary typing (e.g. 1/4) to fraction symbols, works for $\frac{1}{2}$ and $\frac{1}{4}$.
Symbol characters with symbols	Replaces characters used in place of symbols with symbols that may not be on your keyboard but that your printer can print. For example, you can replace (TM) with the trademark symbol, ™. Word can display and print symbols if you have installed a screen font and a printer font that contain those symbols. If you have only the printer font, the symbols will be printed properly but may not appear correctly on the screen
Bold and _underline_ with real formatting	Removes the * and _ symbols often used in e-mail and emboldens or italicises the text
Internet and network paths with hyperlinks	Creates a hyperlink when a URL address (Internet path) is keyed in

Preserve

Styles   Retains existing styles when Word automatically formats the document

Always AutoFormat

Plain text WordMail documents   Applies autoformatting to documents received by WordMail

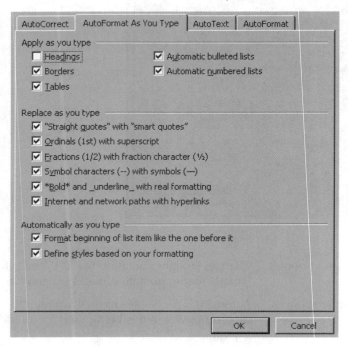

To display the AutoFormat As You Type settings use **Tools-AutoCorrect** and click on the **AutoFormat As You Type** tab. Many of the options that can be set for AutoFormat can be set for AutoFormat As You Type. Some of the typing aids you may set are listed in the following table.

Apply as you type

Borders   If you type three or more hyphens (-), under-score characters (_), or equals signs (=) and press *Enter* Word will replace them with thin, thick or double line bottom border style

Tables   If you type a combination of plus signs and hyphens (+-----+------+--------+) Word will convert them to a table with the columns indicated by the plus signs

Automatic bulleted lists   If you type an asterisk (*), a lower case o, a greater than symbol (>), or a hyphen (-) fol-lowed by a space or a tab and then some text

Word will convert this to a bulleted list

Automatic numbered lists | This is similar to bulleted lists except that if you type a number followed by a tab and then some text Word will convert the text to a numbered list

The options in the **Replace as you type** section are as for AutoFormat.

Automatically as you type

Format beginning of list item like the one before it | If the point, first word or first phase is formatted in a different way from the following text, to make it stand out, then Word applies this formatting to subsequent points

Using the AutoFormat command

By default, the AutoFormat command applies a style to each paragraph currently formatted with the Normal or Body Text styles. Also by default, Word preserves any styles, such as list or heading styles, you have previously applied to the document.

If you want Word to ignore previously applied styles and format your document with appropriately chosen styles, choose **Tools-Options**, and in the **AutoFormat** tab, clear the **Styles** check box in the **Preserve** section. The next time you use the AutoFormat command, Word will apply the built-in styles.

To format text automatically

1   to format the entire document, position the insertion point anywhere in the document. To format a selection, select the text you want to format

2   choose **Format-AutoFormat**. Select the 'Autoformat now' option. Choose **General document** as a guide for formatting. Word reformats the document analysing the text and applying styles from the attached template. Word formats the document or selected text according to the options you selected on the AutoFormat section of the **Options** dialog box (**Tools** menu). If you do not want to preserve the new formatting then you may use **Edit-Undo** to return to the original formatting.

To format text and then review the changes

1   select the document or part of document that you want to reformat. Choose **Format-AutoFormat** and select the 'Autoformat and review each change' option

2   choose **General document** as a guide for formatting

3   Word then displays the AutoFormat dialog box. Click on **Accept All** to accept all the changes, **Reject All** to reject all the changes, **Review Changes** to accept some changes and reject others, and **Style Gallery** to select a different template

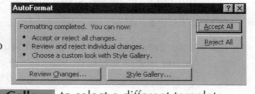

4 choosing **Review Changes**
displays the Review **AutoFormat**
Changes dialog box. Use the
Find buttons to move through
the document and review the
formatting changes. If the dialog
box needs moving, drag it by its title bar

5 Word describes the selected change in the **Review AutoFormat Changes** dialog
box. To make alterations to styles use the style list box on the formatting toolbar.
Do any of the following

To	Do this
Undo the displayed change	Choose the **Reject** button
Undo the last rejected change	Choose the **Undo** button
Display the document as it will appear if you accept all remaining changes	Choose the **Hide Marks** button
Redisplay the change markings	Choose the **Show Marks** button

6 When you have finished click on **Cancel** and then click on **Accept All** .

7 If you decide to undo all changes after you've chosen the **Accept All** button
to close the AutoFormat dialog box, click the **Undo** button on the standard
toolbar.

Note: The AutoFormat command does not format Word tables. The automatic formatting of tables, using the **Table-Table AutoFormat** command was discussed in
Unit 11.

Task 1: Style formatting

In this task the Autoformat command will be used to apply a heading style and to
adjust spacing between paragraphs. Create the text used in Task 3 of Unit 5
(**Centre**) without any formatting and use a blank line between paragraphs.

1 Choose **Format-AutoFormat**.

2 Word displays a dialog box asking you to confirm that you want to format the
document. Select the '**AutoFormat now**' option and the general document style,
and click on **OK** . Word analyses the text and applies styles from the attached
template.

3 Note the styles that have been applied, Heading 1 for the heading and Body Text
for the rest of the text. Select one of these paragraphs and use **Format-Style** to
investigate the effect of AutoFormat. What paragraph spacing has Word applied?

Task 2: Correcting 'bad' word processing using AutoFormat

In this task the effect that AutoFormat has on 'bad' word processing, i.e. text that has a new line at the end of each line and the use of spaces to line up columns, is examined. Create the text used in the previous task but do not use word wrap; force each new line by pressing *Enter*.

1   Choose **Format-AutoFormat**. Select the '**Autoformat now**' option and general document style, and click on **OK** to autoformat the document.

2   As before styles will have been applied and the paragraph marks at the end of each line removed.

Task 3: Bullet and numbered list formatting as you type

First check that the options Automatic bulleted lists and Automatic numbered lists in the AutoFormat As You Type section of the **Options** dialog box are ticked.

1   Key in the text of **Findings** (created in Unit 4).

2   When you reach the first bulleted point type an asterisk, a space and the rest of the sentence.

3   When you press *Enter* Word automatically converts your typing into a bulleted list. You can continue to enter the rest of the points. Note that you may reject this type of change in circumstances where it is inappropriate either via the Office Assistant or using Undo.

4   Repeat this task for the numbered list **Fattips** (also created in Unit 4). For the first point type the number, a space and the text for the point. What happens when you press *Enter*?

Task 4: Reviewing changes

The document used for this task, 'The dialog boxes', is shown below, but for best effect use the disk version, which does not contain smart quotes.

1   Load the document **Dialog**. Choose **Format-AutoFormat**, select the 'Autoformat and review each change option' and general document formatting. Click on **OK** .

2   When the autoformatting is complete click on **Review changes** .

3   Click on **Find ➡** and note in the description box that the first change was the application of the Heading 1 style.

4   Click on **Find ➡** and each time note the description of the change.

THE DIALOG BOXES

Windows applications use dialog boxes to request information from you and to output information that is not a part of the normal data display. Another type of box, the message box, is used when displaying error messages and warnings to the user. If a menu item is followed by three periods (...), that means it displays a dialog box.

Dialog boxes contain one or more special features, or controls. Dialog boxes can support any of five types of controls, these are command buttons, option buttons, check boxes, list boxes and text boxes.

Command button

A command button looks like a labelled button. Examples include the OK and Cancel buttons. If the label ends with a periods, clicking the button will activate another dialog box. If the button contains an underlined letter, it can be activated from the keyboard using the combination ALT-Letter.

Option buttons

A round button (or "radio button") that permits you to select only one item from a group. The button is displayed as a small circle. You can select the desired button with a mouse or use the direction keys and the Spacebar.

Check box

A toggle that turns a feature or state either on or off. The toggle is displayed as a small square which is either blank or has a tick in it. It can be toggled by pointing and clicking with the mouse or pressing the Spacebar.

List box

A box showing multiple choices, such as the Look in list box on the Open dialog box. With a list box, use the mouse or direction keys to highlight your selection and then double-click, or press Enter, or click the OK button. You can also press any letter to move the highlight to the first selection starting with the letter. For long lists, the control has a vertical scroll bar at the right that simplifies movement to the item required. In small dialog boxes with long lists, a drop-down list box is used to conserve space. The list is opened from a single line list box with an arrow in a square box at the right. Click on this arrow to open the box. Then select with a mouse. From the keyboard, hold down the ALT key and then press the down arrow to open the box, select the option with the direction keys and press ALT+down arrow again.

Text box

A box for entering text data. When it is selected, an insertion point appears in the box. You can enter or edit the text before pressing Enter or clicking on OK.

You can use either the mouse or keyboard to move about in a dialog box and choose controls. The dialog box displays default settings. To select a control with a mouse, click it. To select a control with the keyboard, use TAB or SHIFT+TAB to move to the desired control. After the control is selected, set it using one of the ways described above. Close the box by clicking on OK to keep changes or Cancel if you change your mind and wish to leave things as they were.

Note: Most dialog boxes can't be resized.

5 Using the **Find** buttons (to move forwards and backwards through the changes) find the first instance of where a straight quote was replaced by smart quotes and click on **Reject** .

6 Find all other instances of this change and reject them.

7 Click on **Cancel** and **Accept All** .

8 Alter the Body Text style to be point size 12. Select the first paragraph and change its point size to 12. Click on **Body Text** in the **Style** box and choose to redefine the style. This change should affect all paragraphs with the style Body Text.

9 Save.

Quick Reference 1

Basic Windows operations

Some readers may not be familiar with Windows 95 and Word may be one of the first Windows 95 applications encountered by these users. Any reader who has not previously used Windows is strongly recommended to run through the Windows tutorial, which introduces users to mouse techniques and the basic operation of Windows. This tutorial can be found by clicking on **Start**, selecting **Help**, clicking on the **Contents** tab and selecting **Tour: Ten minutes to using Windows**. This appendix briefly summarises some of the key operations and should act as a ready reference to some of the terminology that is used elsewhere in the book.

Mouse techniques

The basic mouse techniques are listed in the table below, with a simple description of each technique.

To	Do This
Point	Position the mouse pointer on or next to something
Click	Position the pointer and then quickly press and release the left mouse button
Double click	Position the pointer and then quickly press and release the left mouse button twice
Triple click	Position the pointer and then quickly press and release the left mouse button three times
Drag	Position the pointer. Press and hold down the left mouse button as you move the mouse to the desired position. The release the button

Mouse pointer shapes

When the mouse is pointed to different parts of the screen, the pointer shape changes, allowing you to perform different tasks. Some commands also change the pointer shape.

If the pointer assumes a shape that you do not want to use, press _Esc_ to restore the pointer to its usual shape.

The table below lists some common pointer shapes as encountered in Word:

Pointer shape	Meaning
I	The pointer in the text area. This pointer indicates where to begin typing

Pointer shape	Meaning
↕ ↔	These pointers appear in print preview when the pointer is over the margin bars at the top or left of the screen
↖	The pointer is in the menus, inactive windows scrollbars, ribbon, ruler or toolbar. You can choose a menu and command, click a button or drag a tab stop marker. This is also the sizing arrow when you have a picture selected. You may drag the sizing handles to scale or crop the picture
↗	The pointer is in the selection bar (at left edge of screen), the style name bar along the window's left edge or in table selection bars. You can select a line, paragraph or the entire document
⧗	Word is performing a task that will take a few seconds
↖?	The pointer appears after you press the Help key. You can point to any item on the screen and click to view specific help
÷	This pointer appears when the mouse pointer is on the split box in the vertical scrollbar
⊣⊢	The pointer is on the style name area (see Quick Reference 3) split line. Drag to change the width of the style name area
↕	The pointer is on a window border, and you can change the vertical size of a window
↔	You can change the horizontal size of a window
↘	You can change the diagonal size of a window
✛	This pointer appears when you have selected the Move or Size command from the Control menu. You can move the window to a new position or drag the window border
↔↕	This pointer appears in Outline view, when positioned on a selection symbol. It indicates that you can drag the heading or frame
↔	This pointer appears in Outline view as you drag a heading left or right to a new level in the outline. It also appears when positioned over a frame handle, indicating that you can size the frame by dragging the handle
↕	This pointer appears in Outline view as you drag a heading up or down to a new position. It also appears when positioned over a frame handle, indicating that you can size the frame by dragging the handle
↓	The pointer is over a column in a table. Click to select the column

Pointer shape	Meaning

 This pointer appears when you select text or a graphic and press a mouse button to drag the selection to its new location, where you drop or insert it

 This is the format painter pointer which can be used to select parts of a document to which a certain selection is to be applied

Basics of Windows

The following are the elements of a basic Windows screen.

Menu bar

The menu bar shows the titles of the various pull down menus that are available with a given application. To select a menu option, first select the menu by placing the mouse pointer over the name of the menu on the menu bar and click the left mouse button. The menu will appear. Move the mouse pointer to the menu option you require and click the left mouse button again. Note that any menu options displayed in light grey are not currently available. Menus can also be accessed via the keyboard. For example, to select the file menu press *Alt/F*, i.e. press *Alt* together with the initial letter of the menu option.

Control menu

The control menu is found on all windows, whether they be application windows or document windows. To access the Control menu click on the control menu symbol in the upper left corner of the window, or press *Alt/Spacebar*. The exact contents are different for different windows, but typically basic windows operations such as restore, move, size, minimise, maximise and close are represented.

Title bar

The title bar tells you which window is displayed. By pointing the mouse at the window's title bar, and then dragging the title bar to a new location the window can be moved.

Task bar

At the bottom of your screen is the taskbar. It contains the Start button, which you can use to quickly start a program or to find a file. It's also the fastest way to get help.

When you open a program, document or window, a button appears on the taskbar. You can use this button to quickly switch between the windows you have open.

Maximize, minimize, restore and close buttons

 Clicking on the **Maximize** button enlarges a window to its maximum size, so that is fills the whole desktop.

Clicking on the **Restore** button will restore a maximised window to its previous size.

Clicking on the **Minimize** button reduces the window to a small icon at the bottom of the screen. When you shrink an application window to an icon, the application is still running in memory, but its window is not taking up space on your desktop.

Clicking on the **Close** button closes the window.

Dialog boxes

Windows uses dialog boxes to request information from you and to provide information for you. Most dialog boxes include options, with each option asking for a different kind of information.

After all of the requested information has been supplied you choose a command button to carry out the command. Two command buttons that commonly feature on dialog box are **OK** and **Cancel**. **OK** causes the command to be executed. **Cancel** cancels the operation and removes the dialog box from the screen. These buttons represent the two means of quitting from a dialog box. To choose a command button, click on it or if the button is currently active, press *Enter*.

There are a number of different kinds of controls in dialog boxes. These are

- **text boxes** are boxes where you are allowed to type in text, such as a filename. The presence of a flashing vertical bar, or the insertion point, indicates that the text box is active and that you may enter text. If the text box is not active, place the mouse pointer on the box and click. The insertion point will then appear in the box

- **list boxes** show a column of available choices. Items can be selected from a list box by double clicking on the item, or clicking once on the item and then clicking on the **OK** button

- **check boxes** offer a list of options that you can switch on and off. You can select as many or as few check box options as are applicable. When an option in a check box is selected it contains a ✓; otherwise the box is empty. To select a check box, click on the empty box

- **option buttons** appear as a list of mutually exclusive items. You can select only one option from the list at a time. You can change a selection by selecting a different button. The selected button contains a black dot. To select an option button, click on it

- **scrollbars** appear at the side of windows and list boxes. They appear when the information contained in a window can not be displayed wholly within that window. Both vertical and horizontal scrollbars may be present depending on whether the document is too long or too wide to fit on the screen. The small box in the middle of the bar represents the position of the currently displayed text within the whole document. You can move to a different position in the text by moving this box. You can move this box either by clicking on the scrollbar arrow boxes, clicking on the scrollbar itself or dragging the box.

Buttons on the standard, formatting, drawing, and tables and borders toolbars

The following table lists buttons that appear on the standard, formatting and drawing toolbars, and shows their functions. As it is possible to customise the toolbars some buttons listed below may not appear on your toolbar. If you wish, you may add them (see Quick Reference 3).

Standard toolbar

	Button	Function
	New	Opens a new document based on current default setting
	Open	Opens an existing document or template. The Open dialog box is displayed so that you can locate and open a specificed file
	Save	Saves the active dcument or template with its current name. If the document has not been named the Save As dialog box will be displayed
	Print	Prints all pages of the active document
	Print preview	Previews the active document
	Spelling	Checks the spelling of the document or selected sections
	Cut	Removes selected text and graphics and stores them on the clipboard
	Copy	Copies selected text and graphics and stores them on the clipboard
	Paste	Inserts the contents of the clipboard at the insertion point or selection
	Format Painter	Once you've formatted text to look the way you want you can copy this formatting to other selected text. Click once on this button to copy one selection, double click to copy several
	Undo	Reverses the action that you last performed

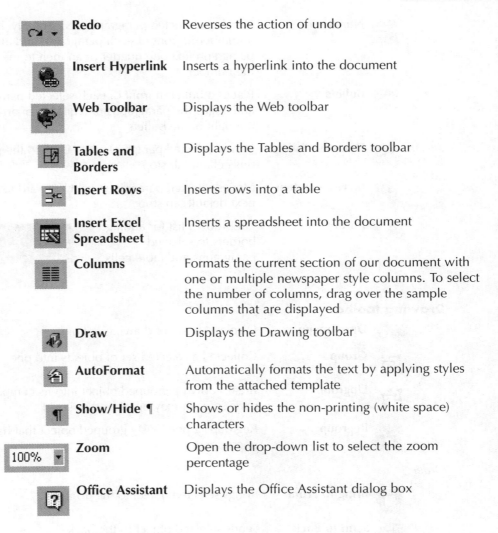

	Redo	Reverses the action of undo
	Insert Hyperlink	Inserts a hyperlink into the document
	Web Toolbar	Displays the Web toolbar
	Tables and Borders	Displays the Tables and Borders toolbar
	Insert Rows	Inserts rows into a table
	Insert Excel Spreadsheet	Inserts a spreadsheet into the document
	Columns	Formats the current section of our document with one or multiple newspaper style columns. To select the number of columns, drag over the sample columns that are displayed
	Draw	Displays the Drawing toolbar
	AutoFormat	Automatically formats the text by applying styles from the attached template
	Show/Hide ¶	Shows or hides the non-printing (white space) characters
	Zoom	Open the drop-down list to select the zoom percentage
	Office Assistant	Displays the Office Assistant dialog box

Formatting toolbar

Style drop-down list box

Font drop-down list box

Point size drop-down list box

B Bold *I* Italic <u>U</u> Underlined Highlight

Align Left Centre Align Right Justify

	Numbering	Numbers selected paragraphs sequentially, inserting a number in front of each paragraph, and aligning paragraph text one quarter of an inch to the right of the numbers
	Bullets	Places a bullet in front of each selected paragraph and aligns the paragraphs one quarter of an inch to the right of the bullets
	Decrease Indent	Moves selected paragraphs left, back to the previous default tab stop
	Increase Indent	Moves selected paragraphs right, forward to the next default tab stop
	Borders	Drop-down list for adding borders to selected paragraphs and table cells

Drawing toolbar

	Draw menu	Displays menu of drawing options
	Group	Collected a selected set of objects into one
	Ungroup	Breaks down a grouped object into its component parts so each may be moved or sized
	Regroup	Regroups a previously grouped object that has been ungrouped

Order

	Bring to Front	Brings selected object to the front
	Send to Back	Sends selected object to the back
	Bring Forward	Brings selected object forward by one layer
	Send Backward	Sends selected object back by one layer
	Bring in Front of Text	Brings the selected drawing object in front of the text
	Send behind Text	Sends the selected drawing object behind the text
	Grid	Allows options for grid to be set for aligning drawing objects

Nudge

Up   Nudges selected object up

Down   Nudges selected object down

Left   Nudges selected object left

Right   Nudges selected object right

Align or distribute

Align Left   Aligns selected objects to the left

Align Center   Aligns selected objects centrally around a vertical axis

Align Right   Aligns selected objects to the right

Align Top   Aligns selected objects to the top

Align Middle   Aligns selected objects centrally around a horizontal axis

Align Bottom   Aligns selected objects to the bottom

Distribute Horizontally   Spaces selected objects evenly

Distribute Vertically   Spaces selected objects evenly

Rotate or flip

Free Rotate   Rotates the selected drawing object freely to any angle

Rotate Left   Rotates the selected drawing object 90° degrees to the left

Rotate Right   Rotates the selected drawing object 90° degrees to the right

Flip Horizontal   Flips the selected drawing object from left to right

	Flip Vertical	Flips the selected drawing object from top to bottom
	Edit Points	Displays the vertices on freeform objects so they may be reshaped
	Select Objects	Displays an arrow pointer used for selecting several objects
	Line	Lets you draw a line in your document
	Arrow	Lets you draw an arrow in your document
	Rectangle	Lets you draw a rectangle or square in your document
	Oval	Lets you draw an ellipse or circle in your document
	Text Box	Lets you draw a text box in your document
	Insert Word Art	Starts Word Art
	Fill Color	Displays a drop-down choice of fill colours for the selected object
	Line Color	Displays a drop-down choice of colours for the selected line
	Font Color	Displays a drop-down choice of colours for the selected font
	Line Style	Specifies the line style for the selected line
	Dash Style	Specifies the dash style for the selected line
	Arrow Style	Specifies the arrow style for the selected arrow
	Shadow	Allows the selection of various shadow effects
	3-D	Allows the selection of various three dimensional effects

Tables and Borders toolbar

Button	Function
Draw Table	Use pointer to drag diagonally to insert a table. Drag inside the table to create rows and columns
Eraser	Use to remove borders and cell lines
Line Style	Select style of line from the drop-down list and draw on the table to apply it
Line Weight	Select line weight (thickness) from the drop-down list and draw on the table to apply it
Border Color	Select colour from the drop-down list and draw on the table to apply it
Border	Select which sides of a cell should be bordered
Shading Color	Select colour of shading for a cell or selection
Merge Cells	Make two or more cells into one
Split Cells	Make one cell into two or more
Align Top	Aligns horizontally orientated text with the top of the cell
Centre Vertically	Aligns horizontally orientated text centrally within the cell
Align Bottom	Aligns horizontally orientated text with the bottom of the cell
Distribute Rows Evenly	Makes all rows of even height
Distribute Columns Evenly	Makes all columns of even width
Table AutoFormat	Provides autoformatting for the table
Change Text Direction	Text may be vertically orientated within a cell
Sort Ascending	Sort selected data into ascending order
Sort Descending	Sort selected data into descending order
AutoSum	Totals a row or column

Customising Word

Word can be customised to suit the particular user or the circumstances in which it is being used. In this Quick Reference the options available from the **Tools** menu will be investigated. The options available from **Tools-Options** are grouped into categories, which are

- view
- track changes
- save
- edit
- print

- general
- user information
- spelling and grammar
- compatibility
- file locations

Not all of these will be discussed, only those options which it is considered the reader may wish to change. To change any of the other options consult the help information and the manual to be sure that you know the effect of any change you make.

View

In this category the options available affect the window display, text and non-printing characters. You may set the width of the style area, which is an area displayed to the left of the document, in Normal view only, which indicates the style applied to each paragraph.

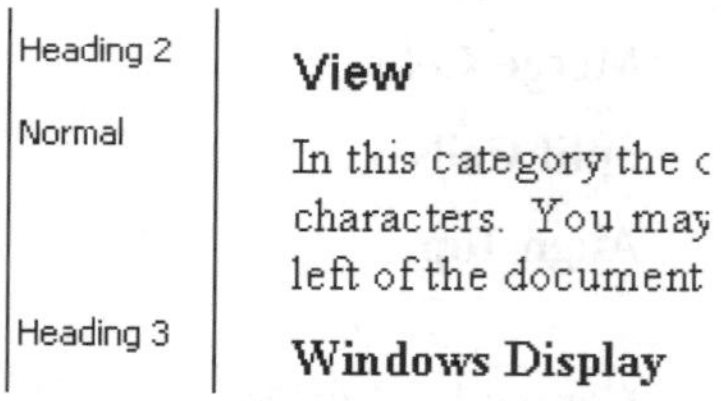

Heading 2	**View**
Normal	In this category the c characters. You may left of the document
Heading 3	**Windows Display**

Window

By clicking in the appropriate check boxes, select whether or not to display the scrollbars and the status bar. Options are slightly different depending on which view you are currently in. If, in Normal view, the **Style Area** width is increased from its default value of zero, the document is displayed with a left margin showing the style name applied to the corresponding text.

Show and nonprinting characters

It is best to leave these options as their default values. There may be occasions when hidden characters such as paragraph marks are required to be seen. However, this is unlikely as it is easy to switch between displaying punctuation marks or not.

Save

Here it is possible to choose between fast saving or creating a backup of your document. It is better to choose to create a backup copy. You should get into the habit of saving your work every few minutes or so. Word provides an AutoRecovery feature and it will regularly save the document. You can adjust the time interval between saves. Sensitive documents may be password protected but be cautious using this.

General

Here you can alter the measurement units that Word uses. You may choose between centimetres, inches, points and picas. You can specify the number of recently opened files that will be displayed on the File menu.

Spelling and grammar

Word can be customised so that it checks spelling and grammar as you type, or not by ticking the options. Options may be set to allow the spell checker to ignore words that are in uppercase and/or words that contain numbers. Through the Custom Dictionaries box it is possible to set up your own dictionary. The Always Suggest corrections box may be used to speed up checking if this is off. Also you may select to check spelling from the main dictionary only.

Edit

The one setting you may wish to alter is that of Typing replaces selection, particularly if you are new to Word. New users of Word can make selections by mistake and if this is followed by, say, pressing *Enter* then the selection disappears. It has been replaced by a paragraph mark. Edit-Undo will remedy this but a new user might not recognise what has happened soon enough. If this option is switched off, by clicking in the check box to remove the tick, then this problem is avoided.

Other settings in this category which you may wish to alter are the operation of the drag and drop feature or the selection of text in units of whole words.

Print

There is one option in this section you may wish to use, which is Reverse print order. This will cause a document to be printed from the last page to the first.

Customising toolbars

If you find you use a command often, you might want to set up the toolbars so they have precisely the buttons you want to use, for example adding the Insert Chart button to the standard toolbar.

To add a button to a toolbar

1   choose **View-Toolbars-Customize**

2   click on the Commands tab, and select a category that includes the button you want to add. The buttons, with their descriptions, appear on the right in a scrollable list box. The **Chart** button is found in the **Insert** category

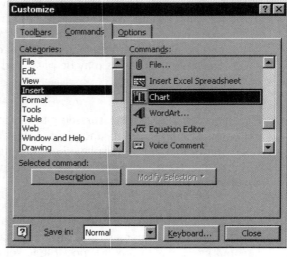

3   when you find the button you want to add, drag it and drop it on the toolbar where you want it. You can create your own toolbar by dropping the button anywhere except on an existing toolbar. You can drag and drop as many buttons as you want

4   when you finish adding buttons to toolbars, click on the **Close** button.

Index